CHAPTERS
OF A
LIFE

CHAPTERS OF A LIFE

JOHN NIEMAN

Ordering Information:

For orders and inquiries, please contact:
1-888-404-1388
www.goldtouchpress.com
book.orders@goldtouchpress.com

Printed in the United States of America

DISCLAIMER

This is a work of fiction. I have done my best to honor historical time lines and events. However, it is not a history textbook. Some names you may recognize—Yogi Berra, Herbert Hoover, JFK, Michael Jackson, Ronald Reagan, Barrack Obama. Most importantly, the meetings, interviews, and dialogues between characters in this book are completely fictitious. I wasn't there. However, I hope that you, the reader, will feel as if you are there.

CONTENTS

For Geraldine,
who has lived through each of these eras.

PREFACE

For the longest time, I have loved to tell stories. In my earlier days, I enjoyed long forms, and would write intricate novels that involved plot twists and red herrings that would later be unraveled hundreds of pages later. Such good fun!

However, after three of these epic and often humorous tales, I discovered a different format: the short story. Perhaps because I myself have a rather short attention span, I have found this to be a very pleasing format. For the writer, it simplifies all those 3x5 cards on the wall to indicate what has been told, and what seeds of information need to be later revealed. For the reader, it provides bite-sized information and assures one that if you don't like this particular tale, just proceed to the next one—which might be funnier or more poignant (depending on your preferences).

This book is a bit different from the previous short-story collections I have published.

It is about one man's life, from 1926 until yesterday. Along the way, we get to know the highs and lows, the career changes, disappointments, triumphs, loves, and passions of Charles "Chaz" Conner's life. Sometimes, I jump eight years. Sometimes, only one or two. Some chapters are lighthearted. Some are heartbreaking. Just like life.

I have written it sequentially. However, there is no need to read it that way. You actually can start at chapter 8. Jump to chapter 22. Turn the pages back and discover chapter 4. After all, they are short stories—with beginnings, middles, and ends. Think of them as episodes. Chances are, if you've been on this planet more than a few years, you've had a few of them yourself. In this case, Chaz had twenty-four of them. Enjoy.

CHAPTER 1

1926: Jazz And Chaz

As eighty-nine-year-old Charles Conner often told his grandson, "The year 1926 was as good a time as any to be born in America. Lots of great music. Dance. Baseball. No wars at the time. Everyone feeling they were in the same boat. Streetcars. The dawn of automobiles. Ragtime!"

Of course, he always left out some of the darker days of the era. Over the decades, he conveniently pushed those bad memories out of his mind. They were too distant, too unrelatable by today's standards—and ultimately, too painful.

And yet the events of his early years were every bit the shaping influences as being injured in World War II, witnessing Kennedy's assassination, burying a son from Vietnam, and every other critical event that Charles Conner experienced during his lifetime.

*　*　*

Since Lucy and Jack Conner had been married in 1923, they tried, rather unsuccessfully, to add a "bundle of joy" (as Lucy liked to describe the birth of a firstborn). At least part of their difficulty was schedule. Lucy was a dance instructor who worked thirty hours a week in a speakeasy on Boyle Street. The place was just one of a dozen illegal booze dance clubs ignored by the police. Here, the off-duty cops could get a free glass of Budweiser, and the Charleston could be enjoyed every night.

While Lucy danced, Jack sang. In fact, he was a rather well-known voice in the Midwest and, a few years later, in all of America. In their early courtship days, he was on the bandstand of McCann's Social Club. Like everyone in the speakeasy, he had noticed the stunning young brunette named Lucy, who was leading a few paying customers in the rudimentary steps of the latest dance craze.

"This song is dedicated to the beautiful brunette who is helping all of our customers interpret the beat through their feet." He held up a glass of beer and toasted the woman. She, in turn, performed a most artistic pirouette, followed by a curtsy. He smiled and felt a flurry of warmth he had never quite experienced in his fast lifestyle. It only took a few weeks for the twosome to become "an item." It started with a few quiet dinners, followed by that Charlie Chaplin hit called *The Kid* at the Fabulous Fox Theatre. Bear in mind, this was before "talkies." As was the limited technology of the early 1920s, there was organ music and silent titles in the grand movie theaters. More germane to their relationship, there was an evening of talk, talk, talk, between Jack and Lucy late into the evening. Both could feel themselves attracted to each other.

Probably the culmination of their brief courtship was the baseball game at Sportsman's Park, where—to Jack Conner's amazement—Lucy understood all the rules of the game, and even know the stats of the St. Louis Browns pitcher George Sisler, Baby Doll Jacobson, and that dreaded visiting Yankee home-run hitter, Babe Ruth.

"How do you know this stuff so well?" an impressed Mr. Conner asked as he munched his peanuts and Cracker Jacks.

"A family of boys"—Lucy winked—"and tomboys!" She then proceeded to reach into the Cracker Jack box and dig for the surprise premium. It was a bright blue plastic ring.

Impulsively, Jack placed it on her finger. Within three months, they were pronounced man and wife at Holy Rosary Church in North St. Louis, and they embarked on the major watershed moment of most individuals' lives— the combination of sharing, sacrifice, twists, turns, and unforeseen events that mark a marriage.

By far, the biggest twist of their union was an entreaty from a Mr. Carl Grunstein, who ran the fabled Goldenrod Showboat. Through the showbiz grapevine, he had heard of Jack Conner, and actually visited the McCann speakeasy on Boyle Street. Impressed with the man's vocal range and style, he began to communicate with him about performing on a bigger stage.

In Jack Conner's mind, it was the opportunity of a lifetime.

"You want to go on the road three weeks out of every month!" Lucy protested upon hearing the proposal.

"It's twice what I make now," Jack answered. With some sympathy, it was easy to fall into this economic promise. The 1920s had all the earmarks of the growing 1950s and the financially exploding 1990s. As with those other decades, it was a bubble—but an irresistibly expanding bubble. If you were lucky enough to be on that wave, it was a wild crest one definitely wanted to ride.

"To deny the opportunity would be stupid," his friends advised him. "To walk away from such a payday would be insane."

More compelling to Jack Conner was the rare chance to make some impact on the exponentially expanding music world. He had heard rave reviews about a singer named Rudy Valley. A guy named Duke Ellington had begun to make headway in the jazz era. And there was this barely known phenomenon named Al Jolson.

Over the past several years, Jack had heard the favorable comparisons with all these talents. However, as a locally based speakeasy singer, he had little chance to compete for fame. As he approached the age of thirty, he began to feel some pressure to make his mark in this world and provide a safety net.

"If we get so lucky as to have a baby, this could provide a financial cushion," the husband countered. "Also, it could offer you the opportunity to raise our kid—God willing—with some opportunities."

There was a long period of silence for this normally talkative couple. She sipped on her Coke. He took a gulp of his beer. For the first time in their marriage, the loquacious twosome endured several minutes of uncomfortable silence. In this stare-off, Lucy considered their relative talents. My god, this woman could dance! But in her heart, it was a faint contrast to the ability to achieve nationwide fame as a jazz singer. Besides that, it was becoming increasingly difficult to be the two stars of the St. Louis speakeasy. Perhaps it was best for all concerned if they had slightly altered orbits.

With mixed emotions, she not only agreed, but encouraged her husband to become "world famous."

Consequently, Jack Conner became the lead jazz singer who plied the Mississippi River from St. Louis to New Orleans for two-week entertainment gigs—two weeks on, three days off; two weeks on, three days off.

At the time, this was the entertainment equivalent of today's Las Vegas. All the big entertainers vied for plum assignments. Louis Armstrong was the head trumpeter, Earl "Fatha" Hines was on the piano, and Jack Conner did the vocals. He was always an anomaly—a white guy in a predominately black band who only sang (albeit, amazingly). He couldn't play the sax or the clarinet or any other wind instrument for that matter. In fact, his only instrument was his voice—but what a voice it was!

The *St. Louis Globe Democrat* called Jack Conner "the greatest ambassador of sound from our home town." The *Memphis Daily News* dubbed him "the warbler on the Mississippi." The *New Orleans Times-Picayune* advised citizens to "Come on along. Come on along … and hear Jack Conner's ragtime band."

It was never really Jack Conner's ragtime band. However, he did seem to be the centerpiece of the performance and garnered many rave reviews. Like Duke Ellington, he sang all the hits of the time—but in his own style, and his own interpretation.

Not surprisingly, this flirt with fame kept him out of Lucy's bed most nights. Even so, it was never a "marriage of convenience." There was love.

However, there was an inevitable sense of separation and a psychological drive for what is, today, called "self-concept." Not surprisingly, Jack felt egotistically puffed about the accolades he enjoyed in every port along the Mississippi. By contrast, the now widely attended Charleston lessons at McCann's speakeasy seemed lonelier than ever. In addition, most of the band members and service staff at McCann's knew that her husband, Jack, had abandoned the place at the height of his vocal powers. To be honest, it was a difficult time to be two independent married individuals on the outskirts of national Prohibition laws.

This weekend was one of those rare three-day stints when the twosome could enjoy life out of the limelight. Jack disembarked from the showboat on the levee of the Mississippi and took a cab to visit his wife on Taylor Avenue in North St. Louis. As was often the case, Lucy greeted him with a kiss-on- the-lips embrace and quickly squired him up the bedroom above the porch.

As always, it was wonderful. Bear in mind, this description is in no way lascivious or suggestive of today's sexual practices. There were no handcuffs. No ropes to bind hands. No threesomes. No cameras with Internet pictures sent across the planet. Nothing like that. Just a very private, loving embrace that ended with pleasure for both parties.

Well, wait a minute. Not so fast with *ended*!

Three months later, Lucy discovered that there might in fact be an eventual "bundle of joy." At four months beyond missing her period, she quit giving the energetic Charleston lessons at McCann's Social Club. At five months, she lovingly informed Jack that she was pregnant. At eight months, he embarked on his next three-week musical tour along the mighty Mississippi.

Within two weeks, Lucy Conner bore an eight-pound, three-ounce baby boy at St. Mary's Hospital on Union Avenue.

At the time of the baby's birth, Jack Conner was singing "Rock-a-bye Your Baby with a Dixie Melody" in Memphis. It garnered a standing ovation.

While he was bowing, Lucy was in the latest stages of labor and experiencing the extreme pain and ecstasy of bringing a baby into this world.

Without consultation from Jack Conner, she named the boy Charles Parker Conner. Partly, she liked the music of Charlie Parker. Partly, she liked the fact that she was a fan of the Charleston, and she imbued the root of that name into her son. Partly, she liked the fact that her husband was a jazz singer, and she might be able to call her son "Chaz," in honor of the dad's contribution to music on this earth.

By the time Jack Conner returned to their St. Louis home for three days and hugged his son for a full thirty-five minutes before complaining that he was "exhausted by his river trips to bring ragtime to America," he was also apologetic that he could not be there for the birth. But in truth, that was not a common practice in those days. Most women bore their children alone in the delivery room, with no husband in sight. According to the times, it was a woman's responsibility. Lucy had already assumed that she would end up being the primary provider for this most wonderful "bundle of joy."

*   *   *

He was baptized on June 18, 1926, in St. Louis, Missouri, at Holy Rosary Church. His name: Charles Parker Conner.

CHAPTER 2

1929: No Blue Skies

On Black Friday, life changed for a hundred million Americans. More to the point of this particular story, it irrevocably changed for a three-year-old named Charles Parker Conner.

There would no longer be fresh raspberries every morning with his cereal. There would no longer be a nightly nurse/babysitter for his mother's job as a dance instructor. There would no longer be a life of optimistic financial ambition for his father.

It was an awful, cataclysmic crash that hit all economic and social levels of American society.

Even with the fresh memory of the 2008 depression, it's difficult to imagine the devastation of the days following October 29, 1929. Within three days, more than 50 percent of all banks closed. The financial loss was more than ten times greater than the annual federal budget. The jobless rate plunged to 25 percent (with another 25 percent working at lower wages or part time). An estimated 50 percent of all kids in America did not have adequate food.

Charles Conner was one of those kids. For months, his mother heated water and Cream of Wheat to feed him on a once-a-day diet. It was relatively cheap, but not particularly nutritious. On the other hand, his mom had even less nourishment during these hard days. Normally, she would spoon young Charles's leftovers, along with a slice of white bread that was rationed daily.

Her husband, Jack, immediately recognized the dire reality of the situation. No, he did not have money in the stock market. But he was keenly aware of the fact that his job prospects were suddenly bleak. Like most people in the music field, there was no easy fallback position, no collateral skills, and no lateral opportunities. Consequently, the "jazz class" was immediately conjoined with street beggars. As a way to stay close to home, the talented singer was relegated to selling apples in St. Louis's Soulard Market. It was a hard tumble for a man who had once performed in tuxedoes with the jazz greats of the times.

Several of his compatriots had moved to Chicago to try to find some paying gig in the Windy City. Most wound up in the streets or rode the rails into the next jobless city. Several simply disappeared. A few lucky ones, like Louis Armstrong and Bix Beiderbecke, had found a way to scrape a living in small clubs. Unlike other unidimensional talents, they were virtuoso instrumentalists. From the ten-piece bands that once plied the Mississippi, they could downsize into three- or four-piece combos and make a few bucks a week. However, in this era of crashed and crushed affluence, it was a meager existence.

Few people had an extra dollar to spend on the "frivolous" arts of music and dance. The showboats along the Mississippi had been shuttered. All the speakeasies in St. Louis had been closed. In the face of all this, who had money for beer? Or for music?

The loss of jazz in Jack's life was almost too much to bear. Perhaps out of desperation, the man added some musical accompaniment to his apple cart. To a few depressed faces, he would sometimes sing "Blue Skies." In a private act of irony, he would sometimes sing "Yes, We Have No Bananas." When depressed, he would sing "Brother, Can You Spare a Dime?" As homage to his current life in the River City, he did his best version of the Bessie Smith hit "St. Louis Blues."

Very occasionally, there was a smattering of applause. More often, the people shuffled past him in an almost catatonic state. In so many ways, it struck Jack Conner as a prison—so many people in a trudge of flickerless emotion.

True, a generous soul would occasionally give a nickel per apple. Other times, they would simply nod and grab a Granny Smith. Unwilling to slap away their hungry hands, Jack sadly and simply sighed and wished them well.

It was no way to make a living. And it was certainly no way to fill the table at dinnertime. Lucy had learned how to bake day-old apples for dinner (along with a little sugar and butter, if available). Some days, she would make a soup of apples and cheese. Other days, she would combine leftover apples with some peanuts, as a dessert.

Deep down, Jack hoped that this would be temporary. After all, Herbert Hoover had said in 1929 that "the worst is now behind us." By 1930, it didn't seem to be the case. There were now six thousand people selling apples in America, and the unemployment rate actually increased.

However, the most lasting challenge for the days ahead was the medical condition that had begun to affect Jack Conner. Perhaps as a result of the winter winds that can afflict St. Louis Januaries, the once-famous crooner had begun to suffer some hoarseness. At first, he thought it was just a cough from the bone-chilling weather. After all, the man had never sung outside for long days in 14-degree temperatures.

But the hoarseness persisted for several months. As a precaution, he cut back on his musical repertoire and started wearing wool scarves around his neck. To his artistic disappointment, it didn't seem to affect his apple sales. It just made the days longer and more monotonous.

In March, when the temperatures began to climb above the freezing mark, Jack began to think it was safe to sing again. In addition to his other favorites, he tried the Jolson hit "Toot, Toot, Tootsie" and the Fats Waller standard, "Ain't Misbehaving." Unfortunately, the hoarseness was still there. In fact, it was now worse. From his once mellow delivery, there was now a definite scratchiness in his voice. Sometimes, there was even a full-stop catch in his throat.

Not surprisingly, this condition alarmed the man who, just a few years ago, was celebrated as one of the great jazz crooners in America.

The psychological tailspin that it created was evident to everyone around Jack Conner. His fellow fruit-stall merchants started whispering that the man was in some kind of funk. Seeing his sour expression, the cop on the beat once asked if Jack had been robbed. However, the one who noticed most was his wife, Lucy.

"What's the matter, honey? Tough day?" she asked him after dinner.

"They're all tough," he tersely responded.

"Well, we can only pray that things will get better," she said, forcing an optimistic smile.

"I doubt it."

"Of course it will. Someday soon, the music clubs will all come back, and you'll be able to regain your rightful role as singer extraordinaire."

This time, there was no answer. The man just looked down at his plate of warmed-over apples, and tears slowly rolled down his cheek.

Three weeks later, Jack Conner went to a free clinic to have his throat examined. After a series of tests, the doctor rendered the verdict that Conner dreaded.

"It's a vocal-chord dysfunction. Something like asthma." "Can you cure it?" Jack asked.

"Not really. It's chronic. But it's not fatal." Then the doc tried to lighten the mood. "Unless you're a big-time singer, you should be able to enjoy a long life."

That night, he wrote his last letter to his lovely Lucy and his dear son, Charles:

> *I think both of you will be better off with a fresh start. Lucy, you are the most wonderful woman any man could ever meet. And, Charles, you have a world of opportunity in front of you. I do hope both of you have Blue Skies in your futures. As for me, I had my chance at life. I just choose not to live the rest of life silently selling apples. Love, Jack.*

Like a million and a half very depressed men during the late 1920s and early 1930s, he left his home and mysteriously slipped into oblivion, anonymity, or death.

CHAPTER 3

1935: "It Ain't Over ..."

"Three things to remember about baseball," James "Duffy" Dumas told his ragtag group of nine-year-olds. "You can't daydream out there. Otherwise, you're going to get bonked on the head. Two: You gotta hustle on every play. If you start doggin' it, then you're gonna be 'boom-bang-bing' out of the lineup. And three: It's just a damn game. I don't want any crybabies on this team. OK? Hey, you come to every practice. You work hard. We all have some fun. And we win more than we lose ... hopefully."

The gruff former marine and first-year volunteer manager of the American Legion team called "The Lions" looked at his prospects with a rare smile. "OK. This half out in the field. This half in a line to see if you can hit a ball."

The regimen and routine was exactly what nine-year-old Chaz Conner craved. It was a chance to escape the grind of grade school at Holy Rosary, where the kid often did daydream. It felt good to be part of some "team." And despite his limited athletic skills, it was a rare opportunity to be some kind of hero—if only with a full count and men on the bases.

Heroes were hard to come by during the Great Depression. There was the bank-robbing duo of Bonnie and Clyde, who captured America's imagination for "get rich quick" schemes until they were gunned down by the Feds. There was the handsome American flyboy, Charles Lindbergh, who helped our spirits soar until his son was kidnapped and brutally murdered. It just seemed that every silver lining was tinged with dark clouds.

And then there was the "Gashouse Gang." In many ways, the 1934 St. Louis Cardinals symbolized the era for many of struggling Americans because of their go-all-out hustle and their humble origins. They were so named by Leo Durocher because of the smelly, dirty, unwashed uniforms— which evoked working-class gashouse guys. It became a trademark of the team, which had decided, as underdogs, to challenge the vaunted, pristine American League teams: Yankees, Tigers, and Orioles.

For a young man like Chaz Conner, such a hometown team was an absolute inspiration. In his hardscrabble life as the son of a widowed mother, the young man listened daily to the thrilling play-by-play on KMOX Radio. It was almost as if no Cardinal player had a real first name. There was "Dizzy" Dean, "Ripper" Collins, "Pepper" Martin, and "Spud" Davis. Led by feisty player-manager Frankie Frisch, the team of soiled superheroes seemed to relish the come-from-behind victories. It was symbolic of the against-all-odd possibilities that characterized the 1930s.

*   *   *

"Keep your eye on that pea. Try to hurt that baseball and drive it," Duffy advised the kid after an eighteen-inch miss at the plate. After two more whiffs, the manager offered another piece of advice. "Try to follow the ball as it comes out of my hand and watch it hit the bat. And as soon as you hit it, run your ass off to first base."

After three more swings, Chaz actually did connect and loft a soft looper back to the mound. Duffy nabbed it with his bare hand, and smiled at the boy. "No need to run on that one. But that's the idea. See the ball hit the bat. And take a good swing."

For the young man, the contact on his next swing was exhilarating. In his hands, the bat felt explosively charged. In his ears, the sound was booming. The ball scurried between the third baseman and the shortstop and rolled into the outfield. Before it could reach the left fielder, Chaz Conner was rounding first base in a full sprint.

"Stay there," Duffy called out and smiled at the hitter. "Good eye. Good hustle." The grinning kid then tipped his hat and grabbed two handfuls of dirt. He rubbed it into his white T-shirt to approximate the rough-and-tumble look of Pepper Martin and the St. Louis Gashouse Gang.

"Next!" Coach Duffy called out toward the backstop, and one by one, they ran through the same batting fundamentals with eight other boys, none of whom were markedly better than Chaz. A few subsequent batters hit dribblers. There were a few foul balls, a few loopers and many swings and misses.

It was the same scarce productivity when the offense and defense switched sides. After a half hour of pitch and catch, where prospective hurlers were identified, the coach called the squad together.

"Everyone sit on the grass," Duffy said. He paced to a fro a few times as the group settled and he gathered his thoughts. "Good first outing. But—and it is a huge *but*—we got a lotta work to do. We're gonna practice every Wednesday at six and every Saturday morning at 10:00 p.m. right here in the ball field behind the church. If you wanna get better and compete, youse guys gotta practice between those team practices. Grab some buddies after school. Newman, Brennan, Kersting, Adler ... it looks like you boys can throw the ball. But you gotta work at it. Aim for the catcher's glove and land the ball in that glove. It doesn't have to be that fast. Control counts. Besides, most kids can't hit that well ... as our batting practice proved. Only three of you got hits: Conner, Welton, Bender. And what's the secret to hitting the ball? Anyone?"

Chaz Conner raised his hand. "See the ball hit the bat," he said.

"Right," Duffy said. "Forget going for home runs. Leave that for Joe Medwick of the Gashouse Gang. For youse guys, just connect. And to connect, you gotta swing. I don't have much time for kids who strike out with the bat on your shoulder. Swing the damn bat."

The coach then looked around at his group of hopefuls. "Practice on your own. Next team practice? Wednesday at six. Get a practice with your friends before that ... and stay out of trouble."

* * *

13

"Practice makes perfect" is undoubtedly an overstatement. Otherwise, each of us could be DaVinci, Shakespeare, Beethoven, and Babe Ruth. Yes, innate God-given talent does count. However, practice does make it better. And it's amazing the amount of progress nine-year-olds can make if they practice pitching and hitting.

After school, Chaz Conner and at least eight or nine other classmates would practice on the field behind school. It would start with a back-and-forth catch just to warm up, and then each player would get about a dozen swings with the bat. At first, anyone who could connect more than a few times felt like a slugger. In a few weeks, most of the boys felt like sluggers. Such is the effect of repetition.

Coach Dumas began to see the transformation in his own practices. Invariably, he raced the boys around the bases to see who had speed. He batted grounders to the infielders and soft fly balls to the outfielders. He tried to school each kid in the mechanics of hitting, and he did his best to encourage the pitchers to "just get the dang ball" over the plate. Jimmy Kersting and Scott Adler seemed most able to do so, and were designated the pitchers for their first game this Saturday afternoon.

"Chaz Conner, Tommy Newman, Dickie Brennan … keep hitting. I can see the results of your practices. Nice even swings. We're gonna need your bats if we hope to score some runs."

The coach then reached in a box and pulled out the official hats and T-shirts. For most of the young boys, it felt like an early Christmas.

"Wow!"

"Red!"

"Just like the Gashouse Gang!"

"Can't wait to wear it!"

In fact, none of the boys did wait to wear it. Out of pride, they all donned their new uniforms. Immediately, they screamed "Lions! Lions! Lions!" and raced around the bases.

"That's the enthusiasm I want to see from each of you this Saturday," Coach beamed. "The game's at three, here … against the Robins. Get here at two." The former drill sergeant then dialed up the passion. "Meanwhile, keep practicing. Practice. Practice. Practice. I want all of youse guys to play. Everyone gets in the game and plays … and try real hard. Remember this: Don't give up. Give it 110 percent. That's more important than a win. You hear me?"

Chaz Conner led the cheers, "Go Lions! Go Lions! Go Lions!"

*   *   *

On their first official American Legion ball game, the Lions defeated the Robins 12–4. Jimmy Kersting pitched and allowed only three runs in the first five innings. Scott Adler relieved and loaded the bases with walks the last two innings of the game, but did prevail. Four Lions got two hits each, including Chaz Conner who actually hit a "triple" (thanks in no small measure to a bobbled outfield ball and a relay throw six feet over the shortstop's head). Still, a three-bagger is a three-bagger—and a weeklong source of pride for the young slugger who had instilled in the team the practice of "dirtying up" their Lions T-shirt to give them some "Gashouse Gang" karma.

For the next six weeks, the Lions won each game—sometimes sloppily. A few of the games were squeakers, but the team had prevailed. With each victory, more and more classmates and parents began to attend the games and cheer every miraculous catch or ground-ball single. It was a heady experience for all the Lions.

"I don't even understand why I wash this dirty T-shirt. You just get it dingy, dirty, and grubby before the first inning," Mrs. Conner told her son in anticipation of the upcoming Saturday game, which was the last game of the regular season.

"It's part of our secret to success," the young boy responded. "It's our good-luck charm, just like the Gashouse Gang."

"Yeah, well the Cardinals better watch their backs. They haven't put the pennant away yet, and the Cubs are gaining on them," Mrs. Conner, one of millions of St. Louis baseball fans, reminded her son. "But I do believe in good luck. So I'm gonna wash it clean and watch you get it dirty when you lead your team to victory, my boy. By the way, you're a good player. I liked that triple. Could you hear me in the stands screaming 'That's my son!' And I'll be there to root you guys to victory this Saturday."

For the Lions, it was their toughest game of the year. In the 6–3 victory over the Hawks, the Lions only mustered eight hits. Chaz was limited to one looping single over the third baseman's head. However, it did mean that the Lions would have the chance to play for the nine-year-old American Legion city championship against American Legion Team No. 8, a.k.a. the St. Ambrose Bears.

St. Ambrose had won the American Legion title game for the past four years. Other than bocce, baseball was the ingrained pastime of this Italian- American community popularly known as "The Hill." The weekly games always attracted a large crowd of locals who would pray for victory at Sunday mass, walk past the front yard grottos of the Blessed Virgin Mary, and then yell their lungs out in support of the Bears.

The game was scheduled for 3:00 p.m. at Sublette Field, the home turf of the defending champs. For the boys from Holy Rosary, it would be a bus ride—and given the interest in the game, another bus was chartered for friends and family.

For the most part, the Lions were quiet on the twenty-minute ride, while Coach Dumas fiddled with the lineup and pondered the possibilities of the game. At this level and in those days, there was no such thing as scouting the opposition. However, Coach had heard from some friends and well-wishers who had seen the Italian boys play. Evidently, they had some two good pitchers who had speed—a rarity at this age. They had a balanced lineup with a few power hitters: two who could actually hit home runs, namely the kids named Berra and Garagiola. Most importantly, they had belief. According to reports, the team just always believed they were destined to win. It was in their heritage. Ir was in their bones. And it was their home field.

When the Holy Rosary busses pulled into the Sublette lot, that field revealed itself to "the intruders." One by one, the Lions walked off the bus and viewed the ballyard as if it were a prequel to *Field of Dreams*. Even in the late summer, the turf was dark green. (Did someone sprinkle it every evening?) There were bleachers on each side of the diamond, and the home- side stands were already filled with fans. More daunting, the vaunted Bears were already on the field. They were wearing full uniforms in green and orange—hats, baseball shirts, baseball pants, and socks.

The Lions, with their T-shirts and blue jeans, approached the field and were gathered by Coach Dumas, who believed it was time for a marine-style stem- winder. "Listen to me. Youse guys are as good as those guys. Better in my book! Hey, we came from kids who couldn't throw or hit, and turned into winners."

He then turned back to the field, which tried a practice 6-4-3 double play. With a squint of admiration, he turned back to his young team. "They think they deserve it 'cause they have fancy uniforms. We don't. We're like the Gashouse Gang. We play hard. We get dirty. We play out every ground ball. We never give up!"

In an inspired ploy, he turned to Chaz Conner and invoked his behavior. "Chaz, how do we play? How hard do we slide? How dirty do we get? How close are we to Gashouse Gang?"

The young boy then reached into the dirt and rubbed it on the clean T-shirt. With his eye on the team, Coach Dumas performed the same ritual on his own T-shirt and then smiled at the boys. One by one, the team did the same thing, and then they started their chant, "Go Lions. Go Lions. Go Lions!"

It was a hard-fought game. By the fourth inning, Jimmy Kersting had held the game close with a few extra-base hits. By the same token, the Bears' pitcher, Mario Margherio, had been equally effective. As a matter of fact, he had only allowed two walks and one bunt signal.

The fifth inning would break the deadlock. The Lions' Scott Adler led off with a hard double between the centerfielder and left fielder. Perhaps shaken by the shot, Margherio then walked the next two Lion hitters.

With the bases loaded, Chaz Conner rubbed more dirt on his T-shirt and swung the bat in the batter's box as the Holy Rosary fans started chanting, "Conner! Conner! Conner!" His mom was the loudest of all. Between the crowd chants, she tried to contrapuntally offer "Chaz! Chaz! Chaz!" as if it were a jazz beat.

On the very first pitch, the kid hit a hard ground ball in the hole. On the Bears' best of days, it might have been a double play, but the ball did have a bit more mustard on it. It rolled off the shortstop's glove, and in a panic, the kid threw it over the second baseman's glove, scoring three runners. With jittery walks and base hits, the Lions ended the inning leading 5–0.

"Don't get cocky," Coach reminded them as the team took the field in the sixth inning. It was important, but unheeded, advice. In the next inning, the team yielded three errors and allowed three runs. At the point, Kersting had thrown three balls in a row. Coach yanked him in favor of Barry Brennan— the hardest thrower of the pitching crew, but the least accurate of the bunch. Fortunately, with his surprising speed, he struck out the next three batters, who swung at fast but out-of-the-box balls.

The seventh and final inning. Score 5-2. The fans on both stands are on pins and needles. With one squib hit and two walks, the Lions have bases loaded and two outs. Chaz Conner rubs his hands in the dirt and wipes off the residue on his already dirty T-shirt as he steps up to the plate. There is a buzz in the visitors' stands without trying to go overboard or rattle this important hitter. However, one voice can be heard all the way to home plate. "You're the man, Chaz," a mother's voice calls out and can be heard by the batter.

The first three pitches are outside by inches, but are clearly called balls.

There is a murmur of disapproval from the home-team fans.

As Chaz digs into the batter's box for the third pitch, the catcher makes small talk. "Great game, so far," he says.

"Especially when you're winning 5–2," Chaz answered back and watched a screecher zoom by on the inside of the plate. The next pitch is of equal speed and nicks the outside edge of the plate.

The catcher fires the ball back to the pitcher and clenches his fist in encouragement. He then turns his attention to the batter. "Hey, it ain't over till it's over."

Wondering what in the world the catcher meant, Chaz watched the next pitch speed toward him. He saw the ball seem to accelerate as it conceivably caught the outside borderline of the plate. As the ball poofed into the catcher's mitt, he heard the umpire bellow "Steerike," ending the inning. The young boy looked at his mom in the stands, shook his head, and took his position in left field—still confident that all the Lions needed were three more outs for the city championship.

Those three outs were hard to achieve. Scott Adler walked the first two batters. He struck out the next hitter, but the next batter dribbled a ball between the pitcher and the third baseman, loading the bases.

The Bears catcher rubbed his hands in the dirt for an extra grip of the bat. He took two practice swings and then entered the batter's box. After two outside pitches, the next one came right down the middle of the plate, and the kid took a full swing. He connected with a wild crack, and Chaz watched the ball fly over his head. He immediately backtracked and witnessed the ball soar at least eight feet above the left-field wall. It was almost as if it were in slow motion. As he sank in defeat, he looked back at the infield and saw the catcher leaping between first and second base. The home crowd was cheering, "Yo-gee! Yo-gee! Yo-gee!" The entire team was waiting at home plate to greet the hero as he skipped toward the plate.

Slowly and dejectedly, the Lions trudged back toward their first-base bench, where Coach "Duffy" Dumas greeted them and asked them all to sit on the bench. "Boys, we played a helluva game. And we just lost by a hair. No one here should hang their head low. I don't want to see any tears. Youse guys hold your heads up high. I'm proud of your progress and your effort. Now line up and congratulate the Bears."

The victors were already lined up between the pitcher's mound and first base. One by one, the boys shook hands and agreed it was a great game. When Chaz met the home-run hero, he asked the catcher why people kept screaming "Yo-gee." The young catcher extended his hand. "'Cause that's my name. Yogi Berra."

Chaz shook the kid's hand and introduced himself. "Well, it was a great hit," the young Lion offered.

"And a great game," Yogi answered.

In the aftermath, all the parents and friends congratulated the Lions for a successful season. Despite all the pats on the back, it felt like the longest twenty-minute bus ride back to North St. Louis for all the Lions—especially Chaz Conner, who wished he had just taken a swing at that questionable 3-2 pitch with the bases loaded.

*   *   *

To lick his wounds, Chaz listened to daily play-by-play of the St. Louis Cardinals, who, by the end of summer, were locked in a tight pennant race with the Chicago Cubs. Of course, the Gashouse Gang had the edge since they were the defending champions and, by most accounts, had the better players. For starters, they had two of the best pitchers, who just happened to be brothers. Between Dizzy and Paul Dean, the duo had forty-seven wins. The club also had the major league's best hitter. Joe Medwick's batting average was an amazing .374—the best in both the National and American Leagues. How could they lose?

However, as the nine-year-old had discovered in his own championship game, anything could happen. Defeat *can* be snatched from the jaws of victory. In the evening games after his homework, Chaz listened to the come- from-behind wins of his beloved Gashouse Gang—often with his mother, who had always been a true Cardinal supporter, but was now a concerned fan. Despite a very winning record, the Redbirds held only a six-game lead over the Chicago Cubs, who had mounted an unprecedented surge. The Cubbies had gone 14–0 over the past two weeks and seemed mystically unstoppable.

"You think the Cards will end up on top?" she innocently asked her son after the last Cardinal defeat and Cub victory.

"It ain't over 'til it's over," Chaz repeated the advice of Yogi Berra.

Over the next seven days, the Cardinals won a few games, but the Cubs could not be defeated. In fact, they won an unprecedented 21 games in a row to end the season and finish ahead of the 96-win St. Louis Cardinals. It was the most amazing sports comeback in the twentieth century. However, the Cubs did lose in the World Series and have never again won the pennant.

It's now been more than seven decades. Will they ever win it again? Can the Cubbies ever repeat? Is it forever a thing of the past?

If you believe in Yogi or the power of miracles, "It ain't over ..."

CHAPTER 4

1941: The First Time

Fifteen is a glorious age to fall in love for the very first time. Thirteen is tempting. Fourteen is promising. But at the age of fifteen, one is no longer a "boy" or a "girl." In fact, most kids at this age resent being called kids. They have a right to this resistance. After all, most young men at age fifteen have sprouted more than a few pubic hairs and have actually started caring about how they look in front of a mirror. Most young women have begun developing their more womanly shape and discovered tampons. And each of these genders has decided there is nothing more fantastic than rubbing one's body (or more) with a willing partner.

Chaz Conner definitely felt these impulses. And the object of his affection? A stunning fourteen-year-old named Amy Archer, whom he met at the carnival in Forest Park. It was one of those annual St. Louis events toward the end of summer that always attracted a large crowd from the river town. Reminiscent of the beloved World's Fair at the turn of the century, there was a carousel, a Ferris wheel, a tilt-a-whirl, dodgem cars, some animal rides, food stalls, and midway games.

Chaz had first noticed her when he was standing at the basketball hoops booth, trying to sink three baskets in a row for a prize. After he had sunk two, he rolled the ball in his hands like a pro and took one step back from the counter. At that precise moment, he gazed to his left and found his focus on this young beauty, who was standing about twenty yards away. Given the afternoon sun, it was as if she was backlit for a Hollywood movie. In fact, she bore a slight resemblance to Judy Garland in *The Wizard of Oz*. All that was missing was Toto and the red shoes. Her dark brown tresses faintly moving in the breeze, her cheeks had the faint blush of strawberry, and she seemed to be looking at him.

"Wow," the young man mumbled to himself.

"C'mon, son. Let's get this game going. You got people waiting in line behind you," the barker gruffly said to the dazed kid.

Chaz took one more look at the prizes on the sides of the booth. Plush tigers, eagles, cardinals, teddy bears—the kind of out-of-the-blue gifts that beautiful young women appreciated. He then took another look at the basketball rim and took aim. As the ball softly rolled off his fingers, it approached the target, bounced on the rim to the left, then to the right, and then arced toward the ground.

When the barker called "Next!" Chaz clenched his fists in utter disappointment and trudged away from the carnival booth. On his way, he stole an embarrassed glance at the young woman off to his left. She was still looking at him and seemed to shrug her shoulders with a "no big deal" pantomimed message.

"Wow," the young man repeated to himself. He then slowly walked over to her.

"Sorry you missed that last shot," she said.

"I think there may have been something wrong with that last basketball. It may have been less filled with air than my first two. Or more filled with air," Chaz answered, as if that were the question.

"My name is Amy," she countered with an equal non sequitur.

*　　*　　*

Must one be young to be "smitten"? I hate to depart from the narrative here, but I am struck by the power of instant attraction and libido that seems to be owned by the young.

Even such a clumsy tête-à-tête is a turn-on at age fifteen. As a teenager, are we more capable of reading between the lines? Once we reach the age of thirty and beyond, do we automatically think that less-than-linear dialogues are only an indication of being daft? Do we listen? Or do we just hear?

Chaz listened to what the young woman said and, for the first time, admitted that his third shot may have been slightly off. He sheepishly smiled. He learned that she was there with her older brother. He discovered that she lived only eight blocks away in North St. Louis. Most importantly, he got her phone number.

Amy also did an instantaneous reconnaissance mission. She immediately assessed that the young man standing across from her was a humble and perhaps even sincere soul—unlike most of her brother's friends, who exhibited bravado every imaginable second. Just as icing on the cake for the young man's benefit, he had a cute smile.

"Hey, sis, look what I won ya by shooting baskets at that booth?" A larger, slightly older teenager entered the picture and presented a bright fluffy teddy bear.

"It's really cute," Amy offered, careful to not gush and embarrass her new friend, Chaz.

"Come on, sis, let's go," the older brother interrupted with a "We are out of here" gesture.

"Hey, were you able to use the same basketball for all three shots?" Chaz asked as they started to walk away.

"The same basketball? What difference would it make for an all-star like me? Swish! Swish! Swish!" The brother chuckled, oblivious to any previous attempts by the young man who was now left in the dust. The brother then shrugged his shoulders as Amy had done in the stand.

As young Chaz watched the siblings walk across the grassy field toward the yellow bus, he couldn't help but see the young starlet look back at him and flash a sly smile in his direction.

"Wow," he repeated for a third time. He began to understand why men and women should at least dance with each other.

Three days later, they shared an orange freeze at the nearby Steak 'n Shake. Wanna picture? Visualize those gauzy Coca-Cola posters from the era, with teenagers dreaming about each other. Substitute frothy orange cream instead of dark icy liquid, and you might understand the magnetic appeal of the moment.

As is often the case, the first date was not magical. Hems and haws dominated the thirty-five minute "get-to-know-you" audition.

Who cared? Both Chaz and Amy gazed into each other's eyes and heard not a word that was stumbled and uttered.

A week later, they agreed to go to the Tivoli Theatre to see *Gone With the Wind.* Of course, Chaz went to the Adler house to pick up Amy and promise to bring her home by 10:30 p.m. As you might suspect, it was an audition. Mom and Dad Adler sat on the sofa and shook the young man's hand with a faux smile. Even the basketball star/brother entered the tableau and suddenly recalled meeting the young man by the basketball hoops at the St. Louis carnival. "That's when I sunk three in a row," the brother said, seeming to rub it in. "Swish! Swish! Swish!"

"And that's how we met," Chaz offered to break the silence.

"Are you a good basketball player?" the dad asked.

"Not really, but I am a good person," the young man answered after being schooled on the importance of this virtue by his mother, who by now was the most influential person in his life.

Silently admiring the honorable response, Mr. Adler winked at the nervous young man and offered an unexpected compromise. "Ten forty-five. Latest."

"You bet!" Chaz answered and squired the lovely young woman down the sidewalk toward their first night of touching romance.

Like most people in America, the young couple loved the movie. Amy identified with Vivian Leigh (especially in her nicer moments). Chaz could not help but want to be Clark Gable. The young couple shared buttered popcorn, a couple of Cokes, and the movie fantasy of the grand embrace.

The closest they came to that was an hour into the movie at the Tivoli Theatre, when Chaz faked a yawn stretch and ended up with his arm around the shoulder of sweet Amy. To his happiness, she did not resist. As a matter of fact, she reached up with her left hand and pulled his arm closer around her neck.

Wow, Chaz thought to himself, or perhaps he had uttered it aloud in his theater seat. Hard to tell. All he knew was that it was one amazing high to feel this close to a beautiful young woman. They continued in this awkward seated contortion until the final credits, and then the two walked hand in hand back to Amy's home.

As he had promised Mr. Adler, he "delivered" the young lady to her porch a full thirty minutes before the agreed-upon curfew. The walk home from the theater was mostly small talk and large heart palpitations. Once they climbed the steps, she asked him if he cared to sit on the porch swing until ten forty- five.

"I would love to," Chaz answered in his best Rhett Butler voice.

Unlike the movie maneuver, this time she actually reached for his arm and put it around her neck. Like almost every fifteen-year-old young man of the day, he did not want to seem too shy for the young woman. However, this was virgin territory for Chaz Conner. After a few seconds of indecision, he acted. He put his fingers on her chin and brought it up to his face and touched her lips to his. It was the most amazing sensation the young man had ever felt. It was so soft. So wet. So willing and engaging ... that is, until her brother's right fist crushed him on the left jaw.

"What the hell do you think you are doing with my little sister?" the big brother screamed, standing above a supplicant Chaz Conner. After a dazed moment, the young suitor sprang forward and body-slammed the bully into the picture window, which crashed into the Adlers' living room. There was glass everywhere. Amy started crying. Mr. Adler was on the porch within ten seconds. By the time he arrived, his hotheaded son was lying in shattered glass in the living room.

"Ralph!" he bellowed to his son. "Stay in the living room. I will come get you in a few minutes."

He then looked at his daughter. "Amy, I think it's time to say goodnight to your friend, Chaz."

She weakly waved and walked up the stairs.

Mr. Adler then walked Chaz down to the sidewalk. "Young man, I don't think you are necessarily a bad guy. I know my son has a short fuse. I understand that. But I think it's going to be best if you don't come here again. I don't want the two of you to get into fisticuffs again. And I don't want to replace a picture window every week. Understand?"

"I do," Chaz answered. "I wish it could have turned out differently."

"Probably just not the right time, or the right age," Mr. Adler said. "But I do wish you well."

"Thank you, sir," Chaz Conner answered, and then he walked down the sidewalk back to his North St. Louis home. Occasionally, he touched his left jaw to assess the damage that the brother might have inflicted on him. Other than the surprise attack and the fact that he was embarrassingly knocked down on his ass, it didn't seem too serious.

The more lasting impact, block after block, was the kiss. Given the circumstances, he realized that he would never have another one from sweet Amy Adler. He closed his eyes and envisioned it in slow motion. It was a great one … and well worth the right cross to his left jaw.

CHAPTER 5

The Early 1940: Drumroll

"Have you heard?" Lucy Conner asked her son as soon as he walked through the front door.

"Heard what? Mom, what's the matter?" Chaz Conner could instinctively tell that his mother had been sobbing. It was not a sight that the young man was accustomed to seeing. The single mother had endured widowhood, the Great Depression, and a constant struggle to make ends meet as a dance instructor—all the while trying her best to keep her teenage son from ever going off the rails. Through thick and thin, she was always a resilient woman, and her son had never seen her so distraught.

"Did someone get hurt?"

Mrs. Conner hugged her son and began sobbing again. "Thousands got hurt, and thousands more will be hurt in the years to come. Oh my god, what is the world coming to?"

"Mom, sit down. Tell me what's wrong."

Instead, she walked over to her radio console and dialed from left to right until she could hear the beginning of FDR's speech. "Listen," she told her son and again brought out her hankie as she heard the by-now familiar words:

Yesterday, December 7, 1941—a date which will live in infamy— the United States of America was suddenly and deliberately attacked by naval and air forces of the Empire of Japan.

As commander in chief of the army and navy, I have directed that all measures be taken in our defense. Hostilities exist. There is no blinking at the fact that our people, our territory, and our interests are in grave danger.

I ask that the Congress declare that since the unprovoked and dastardly attack ... a state of war has existed between the United States and the Japanese Empire.

Lucy Conner slowly walked over to the waist-high radio console and turned the set off. "It's awful," she said with a sigh. "We're in for some tough years."

"Well, we got each other, and that's a good thing," Chaz answered, trying to sound older than his sixteen years. "No one can beat us. No one."

The mother then walked over to her son and gave him an extra-long, extra- strong hug. It was almost as if she didn't want to let go. "You're a good boy. I don't want anything bad to ever happen to you."

"It won't."

Lucy just shook her head and looked at the floor. "You're all I got. You gotta promise me to do well in high school. Work hard. I don't want you to end up in some trench holding a gun ... and dodging bullets."

At least for the next few years, that would not happen. The main reason: Chaz was just too young to enlist in the army. The second reason was the promise that he had just made to his mother. Indeed, the young man did devote himself to easing his mom's worries and applying himself in school. If nothing else, it was a refuge from the daily horrors of war.

In many ways, Beaumont High School was a cocoon of social growth and educational development for Chaz Conner and more than three thousand other students. At the time, it was one of the most beautiful and desirable schools in North St. Louis. Located on Natural Bridge Road and just a ten- minute bus ride from his home on North Taylor, the school boasted three stories of classrooms and a wide array of clubs and sports activities.

Four languages were taught—French, German, Italian, and Spanish (Chaz opted for German). The place had a reputation for outstanding baseball teams and was a highly regarded "feeder system" for the major leagues. Despite an enduring interest in the sport, Chaz decided to watch the games and cover the contests for the school newspaper (he became the sports editor). In addition, there were dances in the gymnasium at least four times a year, and the young man attended them all. He excelled at the Lindy Hop, thanks to his mother's tutelage.

However, for Chaz, it was not all fun and games.

Ever since he had listened to that broadcast from FDR, the young man had become less insular about his own daily giggles. Unlike most of his classmates, he read the *St. Louis Globe Democrat* every night after school to keep tabs on the hostilities overseas. Yes, there was some talk about the war at Beaumont High, but most kids were interested in recess, minimal homework, and the extracurricular activities. Chaz was in no way a stick in the mud, but he was more aware of the troubles abroad.

In addition, he had opted to work part-time to ease the financial strain on the Conner household. After asking the local grocer for weeks, he was able to secure a job as a bagger and delivery boy on the weekends. It didn't pay much—a few dollars a day—but it did help keep some food on the Conner table and reassure his mom that her only son was safe and sound even when he was not in the house.

This particular work experience demonstrated to the young man that the war effort was a universal American responsibility. Often, he delivered groceries to North St. Louis wives who had husbands on the war front. Occasionally, he met middle-aged parents whose sons had volunteered for the infantry. In every case, he could sense the anxiety on the part of his neighbors, and he could easily extrapolate that to his own mother's apprehension about the years ahead.

The young man did his best to reassure his mom that everyone would be safe in the Midwest—thousands of miles from the oceans and the battle lines. Of course, that was not her concern. Like all parents, her fear was that her only son would end up in uniform. She completely understood that in this war effort, Uncle Sam needed everyone. For that reason, she had taken a low- paying job at the small-arms plant off Locust Street. It was depressing work inside a dark factory, but in her mind, perhaps that could be the family's contribution. Better her, she figured, than her only son.

A watershed moment came to the young man the next year. Two of his neighborhood buddies—Scott Samuels and Billy Welton—had fudged their age and enlisted in the army. They were two of nine million young men who had volunteered in 1943. Chaz admired their moxie, and he couldn't help but believe that it was a heroic, patriotic act.

He proudly told his mother of his seventeen-year-old friends' unselfish move and carefully watched her reaction. Not surprisingly, she buried her head in her arms and silently trembled. For the past few years, she had admired her son's interest in America's fight, but had dreaded the moment when he wanted to risk his life.

"Not until you are eighteen," she firmly told her son. "Not a day before."

Chaz raised his hand in rebuttal. "Mom, you raised me to be a responsible guy. I just want to do my part."

"Not until you are eighteen," she repeated with even more emphasis. Hearing her laserlike command, the young man looked at her with love and smiled in agreement. Meanwhile, Lucy Conner went to mass every subsequent morning at Holy Rosary and prayed that the war would end before her dear son would have to put on a uniform.

While her prayers may have had the benefits of grace, her proposed timetable to the Almighty was not answered. By the time Chaz neared his graduation from Beaumont High School and his eighteenth birthday, the war in Europe was in full explosive force. In fact, the outcome was very much in doubt. The Germans had occupied southern France. The Soviets had countered, breaking into Hungary and Romania. The US had landed and then controlled Sicily. Subsequently, the Germans seized control of Rome. At least once a week, Lucy and her son talked about the ebb and flow.

As Chaz finally admitted to his mom, it was a strange time to be "at home." The young man extended his hand across to his mother and told her, "I would love to defend the wonderful way of life you have created for me. And I think you raised me to know that this is right." After a pause, he added, "I will be eighteen next week."

With complicated, mixed emotions of pride and fear, Lucy silently rode the bus with her son to the Selective Service Office on Grand and Washington. When her eighteen-year-old entered the building, she paced on the street corner and hoped that some medical fluke might prevent her son from dodging bullets in Europe. Inherently, she knew better. The kid was healthy as could be and would surely pass any routine physical.

After ninety minutes, Chaz bounded out of the civil service office waving a white paper above his head. He looked for his mother across the street and raced across Washington Avenue to give her a big bear hug.

"I'm in," he told her.

"When?" Lucy asked tentatively.

"Four weeks from now, I get to report to Fort Leonard Wood basic training!"

After a pause, the mother responded as she knew she must. "I am proud of you … as always."

*   *   *

Twenty-three days later, Lucy and Chaz had their last meal together as mom and dependent son.

Given the stakes, it was a rare splurge at Kemoll's Restaurant on North Grand, just blocks from Sportsman's Park, where the St. Louis Cardinals competed for pennants every year. Over chicken parmesan and veal piccata, the two of them talked about anything but the war front. Mom reminisced about his grade-school exploits, her son's fascination with the Gashouse Gang, and that one vacation they had taken together in the Lake of the Ozarks. Chaz complimented his mother on her faith and unselfishness. He was particularly grateful for his First Communion celebration, when she seemed to invite the entire neighborhood for a homemade buffet and took every Kodak picture she could in her camera. He also made her mother laugh about the day they went to the Chain of Rocks amusement park, and he held on to her for dear life on the death-defying roller coaster.

"Unlike now, you were so scared," she editorialized. She then looked around the dining room and held her finger in the air. "Waiter!" she called out. "Two glasses of wine! Pinot Grigio."

As soon as the waiter left, Chaz whispered to the woman across the red- checkered tablecloth. "Mom, I'm only eighteen. I don't know that they will serve me."

"If they don't, I will create a ruckus like they have never seen at Kemoll's. If you're gonna go over to Europe and save America, you may as well have any kind of wine or liquor you want."

After sips of vino and bites of tiramisu, Mrs. Conner handed her boy a small rectangular gift. The young man opened it and discovered a beautiful blue Waterman fountain pen. Mrs. Conner had saved her money for such a gift for years. Despite the fact that it was something of an extravagance, she fully believed that it might have special meaning for her son.

"I think you like to write," Lucy told her son. "I want you to send me a message every week. Tell me what's going. Tell me you are safe. Tell me you miss me. Tell me what you fear and what you hope. Most of all, I just want to hear your words."

Chaz rotated the pen in his right hand and then walked around the table to kiss his mother, his protector, his inspiration, and his forever supporter.

"I promise," the eighteen-year-old, on the verge of sudden manhood, answered.

CHAPTER 6

1944: Over There

1/3/44

Dear Mom,

Well, here I am in Fort Leonard Wood, along with hundreds of other recruits who are anxious to save the free world from the bad guys. You would be proud of me. I have to make my own bed every morning perfectly. No wrinkles are allowed. My boots must be shined so you can see your face in the toe. I have turned into a responsible young man, but that's the way I was raised!

Most of the day, we march, march, march … and are told what lowly creatures we are from Sergeant Branstead, who uses more profanity than any human being I have ever met. "Get in line, you grunt recruits. Chin up, chest out—otherwise you are a bunch of ——bags!" I understand and accept that it's all part of the plan to make us a cohesive unit.

You would probably not recognize me. My head is shaved and shiny like a cue ball, but it's the same for everybody. The maneuvers that we practice have already started to sculpt my body. I am sure I have lost a few flabby pounds and put on a few muscles … no thanks to the food, which is "mess- hall" horrid. I miss the veal picatta at Kemoll's; but more than that, I miss you. However, I know I am in the right place. I am proud to be here and feel a sense of honor and duty I could only imagine weeks ago.

Please don't worry about me. As promised, I will write you often with the magnificent fountain pen you gave me. Hopefully, my penmanship will get better with each letter. Meanwhile, keep smiling. When I close my eyes, I can see your face, and it makes me happy.

Your loving son,
Chaz

1/12/43

Dear Mom,

I don't know if things are getting easier, or I'm just becoming better conditioned. We just ran three miles today, and I ended up in the top 10 percent of time trials. One downside: I will probably be put in a more physically accelerated unit, so I will be expected to better my time this week just to keep up. I suppose there is a life lesson here. The better you perform, the more is expected of you.

I have made some friends here. Most of the guys are from the Midwest. Despite some twangs from Kentucky, Kansas, and Oklahoma, we all get along like brothers. We are all in the same boat.

I just wanted to let you know that I am thinking of you. I know you are working in the small-arms plant for the war effort (Hooray for you!) … but I hope you still have some time to cut the rug. You are better than Ginger Rogers. I remember you teaching me a few steps for high school dances; and if you remember in my Beaumont yearbook, I was dubbed "best dancer in the senior class." Thanks to you.

Of course, there is no dancing at Fort Leonard Wood, but my sense of rhythm serves me well when I march.

I am doing well and feeling like an important factor in America. I hope St. Louis is treating you well.

Your loving son,
Chaz

1/28/44

Dear Mom,

I missed a week, but there is no need to fret. I've just been busy with all the maneuvers and basic training.

I have learned to shoot a rifle. I know it is not your favorite activity, but given the world's crisis, I believe it is a necessary practice, if only for self- defense. No, let me be more honest. I need to know how to do this with some precision and confidence. Besides, it's part of the program.

For the most part, we shoot paper targets nailed to trees. We run. We drop to our knees. Then we shoot. At the risk of sounding egotistical, I am pretty good at it. It's just hand-eye coordination … at least at this point.

I feel more a part of a team than I have ever experienced since my American Legion baseball squad. Remember when I took that third strike in the ninth inning?

That will never happen again. I will have my finger on the trigger and succeed.

As I reread this, I worry that you may worry. Don't. I still gain lots of laughs with my fellow privates, and I miss you immensely and want you to feel proud of me in the neighborhood.

Your loving son,
Chaz

P.S. Is my penmanship with this wonderful Waterman getting better?

2/18/44

Dear Mom,

I am out of the woods and had spaghetti in a red sauce (yum, yum, yum) this afternoon, in honor of my first assignment out of boot camp. I was hoping I might be able to visit St. Louis for a few days before deployment overseas, but given the needs of the war, that's just not going to happen. Too many needs overseas.

Why the spaghetti? It was provided to me as a taste of my next destination. I am going to Italy, near Anzio, with about twenty of my fellow infantrymen. Evidently, troops landed successfully there several weeks ago, and they could use our support. We are trained to do that, and I am not afraid. As a matter of fact, I am looking forward to actual action. Enough practice!

Just so you don't worry (and I know you do), it's a secure area. Otherwise, why would they send rookies like me over there?

The next time you hear from me, I will be in Italy. I look forward to it, and hope you are proud of me. Say hi to my friends in the neighborhood.

Your loving son,
Chaz

3/1/44

Dear Mom,

I have landed in Italy and am feeling quite cosmopolitan. What a beautiful, but war-torn country.

I have been assigned to a troop that is a fair mix of seasoned regulars and a few first-timers like myself. They treat me well and make me feel like a valuable member of the team. By day, we try to gain a few miles in our march northward. We rarely run into gunfire, perhaps because we are very careful to clear up to thirty miles for any possible enemies. So far, I have not heard a single shot. However, rest assured, I am always prepared to hear one and defend myself.

In St. Louis, I hope you are hearing that we are "winning" the war. I feel that, but I don't know whether it is just our spirit-building cheer. I'll be honest. Most of my fellow soldiers think it's going our way. All of them feel we are fighting the just, righteous cause. Consequently, we all feel like heroes. It's a good feeling …

even when we get lonely. All of my fellow soldiers do. All of them have family back home—whether it's Maryland, Georgia, Arkansas, Colorado, or Missouri. As I write this letter, my friend Marc Obie asked to me say hi to you from him. I asked him to say hi to his mother from me. That's the power of being part of a company of more than one man. But there is only one mom. And I want you to know that you are the best one I could ever dream of having. Be brave. Keep the faith.

Your loving son,
Chaz

6/4/44

Dear Mom,

Over the past week, we liberated Rome. Our air intelligence led us to believe that the enemy was in retreat. Fortunately, that was true. We marched across the Italian fields and occasionally encountered some abandoned trenches, but no weaponry or gunfire. Even so, we are very careful.

By the time we reached Rome, we all felt safe. What a stunning city. And as beautiful as the buildings are, the women are even more beautiful. *Sono bella!* We all enjoyed bowls of spaghetti tonight in the city. I must say that the townspeople, despite being under Mussolini's thumb for decades, have treated us as conquering heroes. We all danced in the streets for hours. Fun!

I'm sure that tomorrow, it will be back to the grind ... but tonight, everyone in the troop feels very happy. I hope you are enjoying the summer. I think of you every day and miss you.

Your loving son,
Chaz

6/7/44

Dear Mom,

I suppose that, by now, you have heard about Normandy. It sounds like a very bloody battle, and I am sure you are worried sick. Please know that I am several countries away from those hostilities and am in no imminent danger. Even so, it saddens me to know that many good men lost their lives in this battle. All we know is that the Allies did succeed in taking the beach, but at a great price of human lives. I don't believe I knew anyone in the battle, but who knows? I think of the parents, the brothers and sisters, the relatives, and neighbors of the lost souls. I know you go to church frequently to say prayers. You might thank God that I am safe and sound, but also say a prayer for the families of the lost soldiers. It's a tough war, but a great cause. I am proud to play my part, and I pray that you do not gain a gray hair worrying about me.

Your loving son,
Chaz

6/15/44

Dear Mom,

I shot a man today.

I tell you this not to brag or imply in any way that this may somehow be a pivotal turning point in the war. After the casualties of Normandy, my incident is just a blip in the grand scheme of things. However, I do tell you this for two reasons:

I have such a good, honest relationship with you, and am not afraid to share my secrets. Also, I don't want you to worry about me (and I know you do every day). If nothing else, this proves that your son is an able-bodied soldier who is more than capable of defending himself.

Let me explain the circumstances of the event. Having secured Rome (and thoroughly enjoyed our celebration in town), our troops were replenished to hold on to that city and push northward into more hostile territory. Somewhere up here, Mussolini still survives. I was part of this mission, along with dozens of other soldiers. Every hundred yards or so, we would run into another abandoned trench, but approach cautiously … just to make sure there were no enemies in the bushes.

After about a mile of this maneuver, we again approached another clearing. We sent a few soldiers to the left and right just to make sure we were not walking into an ambush. The guy on the left waved ferociously, signaling trouble. Almost immediately, three Italian soldiers rose out of the hidden trench, with rifles ready to fire. A few of us saw them and aimed in retaliation. I aimed at the guy in the middle. One shot, and I saw him immediately, lifelessly slump down back into the trench. Along with my fellow soldier, I took a few other shots. In the end, I know that all three adversaries disappeared below the line. Meanwhile, we saw about six other enemies scurry for the hills. Retreat. Retreat. Retreat.

After a few minutes of silence, our sergeant claimed victory and advised us to walk back to Rome and gain reinforcements. Consequently, I never actually witnessed the dead bodies in the trench (and I am thankful that I didn't). However, I did see the effect of my bullet.

I remember in boot camp when Sergeant Branstead told us that the enemy was a bastard, and cautioned us that it was either "him or me." That's why he advised us to gain precision with our rifles. "One day, you will f—— need it. Yesterday was that day. Thank you, Sergeant Branstead! Thank you, Mom, for raising me to be on the good side of this battle.

Don't worry. I am safe.

Your loving son,
Chaz

6/25/44

Dear Mom,

I was promoted today. From now on, you must address your letters to Corporal Charles Conner, USA. (La-di-dah!) I guess they appreciate me in this US Army. Consequently, I will be asked to inspire and keep at least twenty enlistees safe from the dangers of war. Not an easy task, given the dangers of this ugly conflict.

I am not sure I am ready for this responsibility, but I assume my commanding officers think I am. So I will do my best. My North Star: I will try to remember how little I knew just a few months ago, and how much I depended on my officers.

Fortunately, I am now back in Rome and simply in charge of getting my men in condition for our next mission. I have come to know all these young guys and admire them. I intend to do my best to bring out their best.

Here in Rome, we do have some fun and good food. It reminds me of Kemoll's, but a bit fresher. Just last night, I asked a young Italian woman named Nina to teach me how to make a great red sauce. I have memorized the recipe and promise to make it for you back home.

I hope you are having some fun. I miss you, as always, and ask you not to worry about me. All is good.

Your loving son,
Chaz

7/5/44

Dear Mom,

My squad seems to have a very good spirit. We work out every day. We run maneuvers in order protect the soldiers on our flanks. We take target practice.

In the interest of everyone's self-protection, I do stress discipline. I also allow for a few laughs … but this is not a war for giggles. Even so, everyone here could appreciate some relief from the tension of day-after-day combat.

Yesterday, I sponsored a round-robin campfire talk after dinner. Each private was asked to tell something about their life back home. Most of them mentioned their brothers, sisters, dad, or mom. All of these young men have good upbringing and miss the life they left behind in North Carolina, Florida, Texas, Arizona, etc. I told them about my amazing mom. Then I encouraged each of them to spend a few minutes and write a letter back home. I hope they do so frequently. I know you appreciate my letters … but just as important, it helps me feel "grounded" about life in the USA.

I wish you could have heard me talk about you. I made you sound like a cross between Rosemary Clooney and the nicest woman on earth—all of which is true.

Your loving son,
Chaz

7/15/44

Dear Mom,

Guess what? Along with my squad, I have just been transferred to Southern France. We all took a boat to Nice and are now on the march northward. I must admit that the Riviera is about as pretty as any place I have ever imagined. Yes, I loved Italy … but this country is breathtaking. However, my sergeant has warned us: it's not that pretty after a day or two walking through the mountains and hearing the German gunfire. I have passed this caution on to my squad and have practiced extra maneuvers with these young men. My major goal is to leave no man behind. I have tried to instill in them that we must protect ourselves—at all costs.

I think I am a pretty good leader of these soldiers. Obviously, I learned my lessons from the master: Lucy Conner. I think of you every day. Please, please, please … do not worry about me. I have fifteen guys to protect me. Au revoir.

Your loving son,
Chaz

7/30/44

Dear Mom,

Another week through the French Alps. Less gunfire this week. No casualties. No injuries. I think the Germans must be scared of us. We are in the middle of the mountains, without light. So this is a short note. Know I love you and miss you.

Your loving son,
Chaz

8/15/44

Dear Mom,

We are now less than fifty miles from Paris. I think we are winning this damn war. We hear some occasional gunfire, but I actually do believe we will secure Paris soon. I can't wait. My guys all want to have some Chardonnay and meet some beautiful Frenchwoman. But first things first. Every single day, we secure the land mile by mile and make sure that there are no casualties. You would be proud of me. I am always proud of you. Let's win this thing.

Your loving son,
Chaz

8/25/44

Dear Mom,

With the French free forces and united Allies, we have secured the city of Paris. Wow! The Germans have evacuated the city and moved a few miles north, leaving the City of Lights to the good guys. What food! What amazing-looking women! Ooh la la. We intend to have a night of celebration and then chase the enemy into submission.

Wait, someone just poured me another glass of wine! I have to get back to the *bon vivant.* I miss you.

Your loving son,
Chaz

9/4/44

Dear Mom,

OK, enough fun for one week. We are now in the hunt into Northern France to hunt down the Germans. I hear them only a few yards ahead. I am constantly telling my squad to be aware of enemy fire and protect their fellow soldiers. We have prepared for this. I am very vigilant given my responsibilities. So far, so good ... but there are hostilities around every corner.

Tonight, we sleep well, and I think wonderful thoughts about you. Soon this will all be over. Soon, we will prevail. I sense it in my bones. But each day is a challenge.

I am careful.

I miss you.

I appreciate everything you have done for me.

Your loving son,
Chaz

9/15/44

Dear Mom,

Bad news. I have been injured.

I have thought about how to get to the point of that sentence for hours, and have finally decided that truth is the best answer.

The good news: I will survive (maybe with a limp).

Let me explain. We moved ten more miles northward above Paris. Suddenly, there was gunfire. More devastating, it was cross fire. We had dug trenches, but the bad guys were on the sidelines and lobbed grenades toward us. Unfortunately, two of my men lost their lives—one guy from Utah, one from Maryland. My grief about their loss has consumed me for the past two days. I intend to write a letter to their parents about what wonderful men they were.

But first, I wanted to write to you. In the midst of battle, I jumped on a grenade. It exploded on my right leg. Evidently, I have shrapnel up to my right thigh. On the plus side, I think I may have "saved" a few soldiers with this maneuver. On the downside, I think I will have a few operations over the next couple weeks. I'll probably end up with scar tissue—so there goes my chance to be Mr. America.

Fortunately, the site of the explosion was not too many miles from the Paris hospitals, which are quite good. The nurses are treating me well and are a treat for the eyes.

I can only imagine how worried you are. Don't be. There are soldiers here in far worse condition than me. I will heal. I will walk again. However, this will probably end my stint in the army. I am told that an injury such as mine normally results in an honorable discharge, since the infantry doesn't need men in crutches (and that's probably what I will require for at least six months). At some point, I will better understand the next steps. I assume I will be home by Christmas … and look forward to seeing you.

Your loving son,
Chaz

9/25/44

Dear Mom,

The medical people here think I am doing well. They have removed most of the shrapnel from my right leg, but now they tell me they must repair some ligaments in my knee and calf muscle. According to them, the first operation must heal before they perform this new operation. They anticipate that operation no. 2 will be by the end of October … and then I will require eight to nine months of rehab, probably in the U.S. at a VA hospital.

I am antsy being in a bed, but encouraged that they think I will be able to dance again at some point. Aren't you glad? I got your letters and your books. Thanks.

Let me answer your questions:

1. No, I am not in pain … unless I try to move that leg. Besides, those painkiller pills they give me are pretty effective.
2. I have seen some of the guys from my squad. Several stopped by yesterday. I like these soldiers, and still feel bad that two of them died in our conflict. They have a new sergeant leading them, but all say they miss me, and the feeling is mutual. They all asked me to say hi to you, since they have heard so much about the world's best mom from me.
3. When will I be able to walk? Probably not until my tendons are repaired in October … and then it will be a slow ordeal. Lots of rehab. But the prognosis is good, depending on the success of operation no. 2.
4. Yes, many people in the hospital speak English (with a very French accent). Out of necessity, I am learning some French (with a St. Louis accent).
5. Don't worry. I am in good spirits.
6. Don't worry. They are feeding me well; and even in a hospital, the French food is great.
7. Don't worry.

8. Don't worry.
9. Don't worry.

Your loving son,
Chaz

10/15/44

Dear Mom,

I have good news, and even better news. I am scheduled for operation no. 2 in six days. The doctors predict I will be a bit groggy for a few days, but they fully anticipate that the tendon operation will be a success. They are so convinced of that outcome, they have planned a return for me to the U.S. by the end of the month.

Quite honestly, while I keep the nurses entertained here in Paris, I am anxious to return home.

It won't be long.

I will fill you in with any further details.

Your loving son,
Chaz

10/30/44

Dear Mom,

My operation was a success. Consequently, I will now be homeward bound. Tomorrow, I will be transported from my Paris hospital (au revoir, la belle nurses) to Le Havre, where I will board a boat for New York. By 11/7, I will reach the NYC ports and be met by US Army officials, who will transport me to a military airfield in New York. My flight will arrive in St. Louis at Lambert Field. Estimated date: November 8.

Can you possibly meet me there? I will be transported back home via an ambulance, but it would be nice to see you when I get off the plane.

Your loving son,
Chaz

11/5/44

Dear Mom,

Here's the latest: I will arrive at Lambert Field on November 8 at 8:30 p.m. Don't be concerned when you see me taken off the airplane in a hospital bed. It's not as bad as it looks. I have told them that my dear mom will meet me there and is allowed in the ambulance vehicle. I have all the medical information for the next several weeks. I am doing well and looking forward to seeing you.

I hear we are winning this war. That would make me feel good and that it was worth the sacrifice. But it will not make me feel as good as seeing you again. Can't wait.

Your loving son,
Chaz

CHAPTER 7

1945: Congratulations!

For Chaz Conner, rehab from his WWII injury was a slower, more painful process than he would have liked. For the first weeks back home, he was only able to venture out of his bed on two crutches for sixty minutes a day; and at that, it only consisted of forward steps that were about seven or eight inches in length.

Fortunately, the kitchen was only about twelve feet from his adjoining bedroom. This proximity afforded him the opportunity to visit with his mom during lunch and dinner, and these conversations were the high points of his day.

Lucy Conner was arguably the proudest and most protective mother in their North St. Louis neighborhood. At least once or twice a week, she would visit Meyer's Grocery Store (where Chaz had bagged and delivered groceries before the war), just to keep the proprietor up to speed on her son's heroism and exploits overseas. At the small-arms plant, where she worked during his deployment overseas, she kept all her fellow workers abreast of the firsthand accounts of Chaz's battle experiences. Even before the war, she was proud of his character and ambition. For example, at Beaumont High, she admired the fact that he worked for the school newspaper and juggled those hours with a part-time job in the neighborhood. Through their years together, he never sassed her—not even part of his DNA.

The feeling was mutual. Without ever directly confronting the issue, the young man was forever grateful that his mother singlehandedly raised him with confidence after his father's suicide.

That episode was still somehow off-limits, especially since Lucy Conner never referred to it in casual conversation. "Tomorrow forward" was a motto she once uttered. At the time, the nine-year-old wrote it in his notebook ten times after losing a crushing loss in the American Legion baseball championship.

Besides, Mom was fun. She had taught dance lessons, was aware of the world beyond the Midwest, and liked to cook. On that last point, Chaz could smell the bacon across from his horizontal position in the adjoining bedroom.

"Can I join you in the kitchen in about ten minutes?" her son asked.

"Can you make it eight minutes?" Lucy answered. "The scrambled eggs will be perfect by then."

"Eight minutes it is," Chaz answered, and began the ritual of putting on his straight leg brace and awkwardly crutching himself toward the kitchen table. He had begun to improve on this procedure, but just barely. What once took ten minutes now took less than seven. However, the remaining hours were endured lying on his back. For a young man who had always thrived on activity, these month-after-month doldrums were excruciating.

As he clomped toward the kitchen table, he sent a wink and a smile to his mom. "That smells great. I wish I could help you cook," he offered.

"It's enough reward to just be able to share a lunch with you," Lucy answered. She then put sustenance on each plate and felt so happy to have a lunch with her guy. "Have you read the papers? It looks like Germany is in total retreat," she volunteered.

"Yep! Read all about it." He then dug into his softly scrambled eggs. "I just hope my guys are all safe."

"They have you to thank for their lives."

"Some of them," Chaz answered. "Some are now gone." He then took another bite of his brunch and shook his head sadly about the losses of war. It was a subject that often bedeviled him, and not just in terms of American soldiers. More than fifty million men from dozens of countries had been killed, and despite some momentum on the part of the Allies, he knew there would inevitably be more casualties in the months and years ahead. "They all had families," Chaz murmured.

After a pause, Lucy reached over and touched her son's hand. "Honey, a war like this one affects everyone. But I thank God every day that you have come back with four limbs and a sound mind."

"I'm not sure about that fourth limb," he chuckled back. "I've got to get back on my own two feet. This lying in bed thing is driving me nuts. I wonder if you could help me get to the VA hospital for therapy."

"Let's do it," his mom responded. "When?"

"I have an appointment on Monday."

And so the long, hard climb began. Over the next few months, Lucy and Chaz took the no. 2 bus to Jefferson Barracks VA hospital and underwent physical therapy on Mondays, Wednesdays, and Fridays. The young man really hated having to ask his mother to accompany him on these trips, but he fully accepted the fact that he was still very unsteady on two crutches. Even his therapists at the hospital advised him that it was not advisable at this stage to walk to the bus stop, climb the steps, undergo therapy, and then repeat the routine all by himself. Consequently, for months, they were commuting partners. Mom and son would split the newspapers and occasionally read the latest novels. Her favorite at the time was *Cannery Row* by Steinbeck, which captured the Great Depression. His was *Animal Farm* by George Orwell, for prescient and allegorical writing about contemporary life. However, on many of the days, the two would talk about anything: spring, neighbors, or the latest radio programs (*Superman, Open House Party,* and *The Saint*).

By April, Chaz was able to walk around the block on crutches with more confidence, meeting the bus on his own. However, it was still destined to be a slow heal. His doctors advised him that it would take until September to feel fully ambulatory. Consequently, the young man began to focus on a more complete life after the end of summer.

The whole idea of "what's next?" consumed him. After the daily preoccupation of simply staying alive in battle, the concept of long-range life planning was a foreign concept to the young man. Three events helped shape his thought process.

The first was an event that happened in the neighborhood and deeply affected his mother. On April 25, she saw two officers in uniform approach the porch of her next-door neighbor; they left after ten minutes. Her instincts told her what the meaning of that private announcement was. Out of respect, she waited several hours before walking to her neighbor's house and knocking on the door.

"Is everything OK?" she asked with some trepidation—and a premonition that negative news was in store.

Mrs. Collins opened the screen door in tears. "My son is gone," she answered. She then collapsed into Lucy's arms in an inconsolable state. After several hours of joint reminiscences about her son's youth, adolescence, and war heroism, the two women shared tea.

"If you are willing," Lucy asked tentatively, "I think it would be good to have a celebration of his life this weekend. I'll make the food and the dessert. You just make the coffee ... and supply the Irish whiskey."

When Chaz came back from therapy that day, his initial response was that he did not want to attend and be reminded of the horrors of the war.

"He could have been one of your soldiers," Lucy reminded him, and the young man immediately agreed to crutch over on Saturday and offer his condolences. As a matter of fact, he even helped chop some vegetables for his mother's favorite chili recipe in the morning and box the homemade gooey butter cake that had become a family favorite.

When they arrived at the Collins house, there were already about ten neighbors there, and that number grew to thirty by midafternoon. Mrs. Collins had placed a selection of pictures of their son in the living and dining room. They ranged from his First Communion and youth baseball leagues to more grown-up shots of Joey Collins in uniform. Yes, in many ways, it was a wake. Inevitably, there were tears and sad memories; but as is true of many Irish families, there was also some gallows humor and laughter about the boy's lighter moments.

With his crutches and limp, Chaz Conner did his best to deflect sympathy from the crowd. "I'm just here to celebrate and commemorate Joey's life," the young neighbor found himself repeating. However, the contrast between the men's fate was indelible to him. One was gone. One had a limp. One would soon be buried. One was in rehab. One's life would be in the past. One must move into the future. That very evening, Chaz began to ponder where that future road might lead him.

The second incident that affected him was the wind-down of the war. On May 7, 1945, Germany surrendered to the Western Allies. At first, everyone assumed that peace would be here in a matter of days. However, hostilities continued in Asia for months; and week after week, more American lives were lost. All of that came to a sudden and dramatic end in August, when Hiroshima and Nagasaki suffered the world's first atomic bombs.

Like many Americans, Chaz had some mixed emotions about these blasts. As someone who still had friends in uniform, he was relieved to think that it may save some lives and speed the end of the war. On the other hand, More than 160,000 lives were lost with those two attacks. Within five days, Japan surrendered; and there was a welcomed, but eerie, silence of gunfire.

For the young man in North St. Louis, the event definitely signaled the end of an era. Wars would no longer be the same. Life would never be the same. Perhaps life after war should never be the same, he began to think.

The third impetus for change was an act of Congress, specifically the GI Bill. Passed in the middle of 1945, its intention was noble: to say thank-you to the more than sixteen million young men who had defended our country during the conflict. It was also intended as a restart for American society and a method to ease the employment burden that would surely befall this country when boatload after boatload of soldiers came home.

If Chaz ever needed a signal that it was time to take the next step forward this bill was it. By now, he had ditched his crutches and begun to walk with a cane. His doctors told him that by autumn, he would be able to throw away that cane and put one foot in front of the other. For the young man, that meant the freedom to pursue the future on his own terms.

The GI Bill made that possible. At the VA hospital, he checked out the procedures and found that many of the benefits applied to him—including educational support, which would more than pay for college tuition. After checking out many of the programs at Washington University, St. Louis University, and the University of Missouri, he came to the conclusion that one place and one area of study were ideal.

At dinner that evening, his mother announced that he had received two letters in the mail: one from the US Army and the other from Mizzou.

While he put the letters to the left of his plate, he helped himself to the roasted chicken and potatoes that his mother had prepared. "It looks delicious, Mom," he said, and began to cut the chicken meat off the bone.

"Of course, it's delicious. I made it with thyme and lemon, but read the letters," she requested of her son.

He opened the rather official US Army letter first. The first word was *congratulations*, so he knew it would not be bad news. As he scanned the single page, his lips could not resist a slight upturn of pride.

"Yes?" his mom asked. "Do tell."

Rather quietly, the young man told her, "Wow, I was awarded the Purple Heart for my actions in France."

Before he could complete the sentence, his mother bounded across the table and gave him a huge hug. "I am so, so proud of you," she announced with tears in her eyes.

"It's a nice honor," he said humbly.

"It's deserved," Lucy said and did a spontaneous jitterbug back to her seat across from him. "You are the best son a mom could ever have. And the bravest! Read the next one," she urged him.

Chaz took another bite of his chicken and took a few seconds to stare at the university letter. To be honest, he had broached the subject of going to college to his mother—but it had so far been a vague plan about finding something to fill his days. Perhaps this year. Perhaps next year. Perhaps business. Perhaps he might study to be a teacher. Perhaps something even more fulfilling. Perhaps he could write.

"Open it up," his mom repeated.

After a sigh, the young man cleaned off his knife and opened the letter. When he read the first line—*Congratulations!*—he knew a conversation with his mom was necessary.

"Mom, you know with the GI Bill, I could attend a topflight university without a financial burden."

"Yes, we have talked about this. But you need to figure out what you want to do with the rest of your life. Remember? So you could maybe go to St. Louis University … or Washington U."

"Or Missouri University," Chaz countered, holding the letter to his forehead.

"It's so far," she quietly answered.

"It's not that far," he countered. "And they have the best journalism school in the country. Hands down."

Lucy quit eating her chicken and beans and looked at her son. "Journalism?" she asked.

Chaz then reached in his shirt pocket and pulled out the Waterman pen his mother had bought for him several years ago. It had become the instrument for all his handwritten letters back home, and his conduit for emotions overseas. He placed the pen in from of his mom's plate. He then looked his mom directly in her eyes. "Your instinct was 100 percent correct. I like to write. And Mizzou has the best journalism school in the country."

"You think you can do it that well … to compete with the best in the country?"

"I think I have the curiosity and the talent for that. And you do too. Otherwise, you would have never given me this fountain pen and encouraged me to put sentences together," Chaz said with no apparent attitude, only admiration for his mom.

"When?" she asked.

"The semester starts in September," he said with an apologetic shrug.

"So soon," she said sadly. "I wish it weren't so sudden, so I could enjoy your company every day."

"I know," he said with some understanding. "But I think I may do well in this field. I think it may be my calling. And I think I will make you very proud to call me your son."

"I already feel that," Lucy immediately responded. Then in a slow-motion reenactment of his Purple Heart celebration, his mother pushed her chair back and walked over to her son. "I am so very, very proud of you," she reiterated to him, fighting back the tears, which would later flow privately in her bedroom.

CHAPTER 8

1947: Fresh Start

Like many young men and women of the era, Chaz Conner was the first member of his family to ever attend college.

He liked the environment from his first day on campus. Unlike the occasional gloom and life-and-death pressure of war, the school was filled with optimists, intent on building their own future. With a similar lack of legacy or privilege, most of his fellow students worked hard. They attended class regularly, did the readings, and normally turned in papers close to the due dates. This was particularly true in journalism school.

The university was the first school in the nation to have a bona fide journalism degree. Unlike other colleges, it pioneered an approach called "The Missouri Method," which combined classroom teaching with real-life, practical experience in the newsroom. The jewel of its program was the daily newspaper *The Columbia Missourian*, which was published by University of Missouri students and was relied upon by citizens throughout the center of the state for national and local stories, opinion, sports, classified ads, lifestyle, and the arts.

Even as a freshman, the paper did provide an outlet for journalistic growth, albeit on a rookie scale. In his first semester, Chaz learned how to sell and design retail ads for some of the supermarkets and hardware stores in the area. Admittedly, it didn't exactly require the high art of writing, but he also was given the occasional responsibility (once every three weeks) of covering the local city-council meetings and filing a report. Given the routine minutiae of these meetings, it was not considered a plum assignment, which is why Chaz gained the assignment in his freshman year.

In addition, each journalism student was urged to contribute essays at least once a month in the hopes that their words might be published in *The Columbian*. Of course, all Mizzou students were allowed to do this—but as a J-school enrollee, the encouragement was closer to an expectation from the faculty.

This interaction with the newspaper gave two social networks at Missouri University. Of course, he had the dorm-life swirl that every freshman enjoys.

In Chaz's case, he was a resident of Defoe-Graham Hall. Here, he enjoyed connections with a wide cross section of students. Almost of all of them were from Missouri, but beyond his St. Louis hometown. Many came from Kansas City, Springfield, the Missouri Bootheel, and more rural counties. Almost all of his fellow students had varied interests—math, education, science, business, engineering, psychology, architecture, etc.

The J-school and the newspaper gave him a network of kindred spirits. Even though he was low man on the totem pole, he was always a personable guy who could deal with peers and those above. In addition, he loved the pursuit of news (or "truth" as he called it, as a young academician). Without overtly trying too hard, he became friends with the assistant editor, the sports editor, and the op-ed editor on his first year on campus. It was not a "suck-up" maneuver. As part of the "Missouri Method," most young contributors were encouraged to practice their one-on-one skills with those in charge … and vice-versa.

However, social life at Mizzou was not limited to dorm life and degree stepping-stones. At the time, it was known as one of the best party universities in the nation.

In the fall, after every Missouri Tiger football game, the town of Columbia overflowed with celebrants (win or lose). Often, the rowdiest parties were in the fraternities, but it also spilled into the streets, thanks to a rather tolerant police force. After the inevitable Bowl invitations, the winter did not diminish the social scene. A basketball defeat could be interpreted as a reason to raise a glass or two.

Other excuses to have fun:

1. January 8—Elvis Presley's birthday
2. February 2—Groundhog Day
3. February 14—Valentine's Day
4. February 20—Cherry Pie Day
5. Early March—Good Friday
6. March 17—St. Patrick's Day
7. March to April—Lent
8. Early April—Easter
9. Every Friday
10. Every Saturday

The combination of educational advancement and social enhancement made MIssouri Univeristy an ideal location for the twenty-year-old freshman. Like most students, he worked hard and played hard. Unlike most of his compatriots, he did earn some notoriety in his first year by having two editorials published in *The Missouri Columbian.*

The first one was written over the weekend after seeing one of the most popular movies of the year. It was titled *It's a Wonderful Life*—at least for some, according to Chaz Conner.

Here's part of the text:

> I am a fan of Jimmy Stewart and Donna Reed, and like everyone in America, I love a happy ending. However, I also recognize that in the shadow of our most cataclysmic world war, there are still millions of people who suffer. For them, the situation cannot be turned around in a two-hour Hollywood fairy tale. These neighbors, mothers and fathers, aunts and uncles cry every night for their lost brethren, lost sons, or people they passed every day down the street. Now they no longer exist. The pain lasts longer than a two-hour celluloid sunrise.

Yes, yes, yes … I know we all need escapism. However, could we possibly balance that with a slight dose of reality? How about a movie that confronts the agony of a lost soldier under one's command? How about a story that tells of the heroism of a neighbor boy and a mother who takes it upon herself to organize a wake of whiskey, wisdom, and wit? I have attended such a ceremony, and it was not a downer. It was downright inspirational! Should I write this script? Or should I stay in journalism and just prod you folks in Hollywood to go beyond the musical swell and the happy faces? I believe in you. Do you believe in yourself?

This particular story was reprinted in *The Hollywood Reporter,* and it did get some positive feedback from Hollywood directors.

However, it was not Chaz's biggest editorial of the year. That was an op-ed piece called "Tel A Vivre (Long May It Live)." Part of the appeal was the catchy title. The bigger impact came from the middle paragraphs:

I witnessed a friend die three feet to my right. I saw another soldier die a few feet in front of me. However, I did not witness six million innocent individuals walk into the showers and be silently exterminated. No soldier, no squad, no troop, no battalion, no movement, no country, no united Allied force ever acknowledged this evil. However, it clearly existed.

Perhaps we had our eyes closed. More likely, we had our minds closed.

This particular phrase was boldfaced and subheaded in most of the reprinted editorials, which include *The New York Times,* the *Chicago Tribune,* the *St. Louis Globe-Democrat,* and *Stars and Stripes,* the publication which was distributed to the millions of military men still in uniform.

In his second year at Mizzou, Chaz joined Pi Kappa Psi fraternity and became the assistant editor of the *Missouri Columbian—* glide path to post- college success. In that year, he also met Leah Carmichael.

In the words of his frat, she was a C&P girl, meaning "cute and perky." In the words of Chaz Conner, she was definitely that—but also one of the most challenging, intelligent, and sexually adventurous young women he had ever met.

He met her at a sorority party.

"Wow, you look amazing tonight," he opened. OK, it was not the most original line in the history of pickup repartee. However, it did have the advantage of being spontaneously honest.

"You're the writer," she responded; and from that minute, he was completely smitten. The young woman babbled something about his essay on the Jimmy Stewart movie, but Chaz barely heard half of it. He looked at her eyes, her lips, her stance, and her body type. Well, wait a minute! Truth be told, he barely got down to her slinky body type. He could not take his gaze off her hazel eyes, which seemed to dance with pleasure and invitation.

That very night, the two of them ended up in an irresistible lip-lock, which would be the start of many evenings to come.

Let's not make this all about sex. Leah was a very bright young woman who could dish it out as well as take it in. As a psyche major from the Psychology Center of Chicago and the daughter of two urban professionals, she was quick of wit and up to date in current events. Chaz's ironic sarcasm never flew far above her head.

Her decision for college boiled down to Mizzou vs. Northwestern.? The University of Chicago never seemed to be in contention for her. As she once explained to Chaz, she had no desire to attend an egghead university, which had zero proclivities for day-to-day happiness.

By the end of their first year, both of them seemed to have a fair amount of that quotient. Rather than go overboard, they both limited their mutual exposure and agreed to see each other a few times a week. However, in April, when spring fever broke out on campus, that artificial parameter became even more artificial.

In addition to their physical attraction, both liked each other's sense of humor and eclectic interests in the world. Their most difficult time was the summer, when they went back to their hometowns and were inevitably separated from each other's embrace. For Leah, it was a good time to reconnect with her family and her friends in the Windy City. For Chaz, it was a crucial time to acknowledge, appreciate, and advance the relationship with his only parent—the woman named Lucy, who had raised and nurtured him.

CHAPTER 9

1949: 3X5 Cards

"**M**om!" he yelled out at twice the normal decibel level when he walked through the door on Euclid Avenue. Almost on cue, his forty-two-year-old mother skipped into the living room and gave her only son the bear hug she had dreamed of sharing for the past several months.

"You look great! You look happy," she announced.

"I am very, very happy to be home," he honestly admitted. As he had matured and become more independent over the past eight months, he had become more and more appreciative of evrything his mother had done and the sacrifices she had made on his behalf. Yes, he always said thanks to his mom when she made him breakfast or took him to physical therapy from his war injury. He had enjoyed his first summer-break Christmas holidays with her, but he somehow felt it had blurred by. Perhaps as a result of his Mezzou classes in researching a topic and going beyond the headline, it occurred to the twenty-two-year-old that it would nice to actually know Lucy Conner better—her drives, her fears, her ambitions, her history. As a matter of fact, he had vowed to be a more interested, inquisitive son this summer.

"I've got a plan for the next twelve weeks," he announced to his mother. "I say that once a week, we go out to dinner and just shoot the breeze … without you having to prepare a meal, or me needing to dry the dishes."

"Yeah, but I like to cook meals for you," she retorted.

"And you're damn good at it. So you get to do it six nights a week, and I get the thrill of drying those dishes six nights a week. But on one night a week, it's like we're on a mom-son 'date.' Not in a 'date-like' way ..." he felt the need to explain. "Are you game?"

"That would be fun." She smiled back at him. "As long as we don't blow our whole budget on the biggest restaurants in town."

"No, a bunch of local dives ... and at least once at Kemoll's."

"Deal," she confirmed.

On their first "date," Chaz and his mom went to Santorum's Pizza Parlor near Washington University. Even in the summer, it was filled with college students.

"Do they look like your roommates? Are the women across this restaurant as attractive as all the beautiful young women in your life?" Lucy asked in a surprisingly forward but teasing manner.

"No. And no," her son answered. "Well, this is going to be challenging," the son said, almost to himself. In an attempt to change the subject, Chaz jabbed back, "When was your last date? How was it? Do you still teach dancing? Do you ever meet a person you want to squeeze?"

Unaccustomed to such personal questions, Lucy took a sip of her Budweiser and answered, "Never. Not applicable. Yes. Not yet."

The "not yet" answer opened the dialogue for Chaz Conner, who—via journalism—had become accustomed to looking for any available opening. "I am assuming from your last answer that you may be open to a new relationship," he projected.

After a few hems and haws, Lucy stumbled on the fact that it had, in fact, been difficult to find a new male friend. Bear in mind, in those days, remarriage was not as common as it is now. "Quite honestly, I have not been looking," she finally said. "Maybe I should. I don't know. I wouldn't even know where to begin."

"Yeah, well, you are still a fantastic-looking woman ... and a great catch," Chaz offered.

The very idea that she could be viewed as "a catch" made her wince. In a series of monosyllabic responses, she said "yikes" then "wow" then "oh boy." Obviously, she had not been quizzed this personally in many years. But as Chaz had hoped, that was the point of "mom-son" dates.

"I don't want to make you uncomfortable," the son responded. "I just want to understand your head better."

"My head? Is that jargon at college?" she asked.

"Yeah, sort of ..." Chaz answered. "Mom, I just want to know you better. And this spring, I thought of all these questions I had for you. Like all my journalism interviews, I put them on 3x5 cards." Somewhat apologetically, he ventured, "It's just so I know how to stay on the topic. I write the subject down ... and we can meander any way and anywhere after that." He then reached in his pocket and pulled out an index card. It contained a handwritten note: "Do you date?"

"Didn't we just cover that topic?" she asked.

"Yeah," Chaz answered. "So it was just an example. A short trial run."

"This is really the way you conduct a journalistic interview?" she asked.

"Sometimes," he honestly answered. "Sometimes I like the element of surprise. But with my own dear mom, I thought that might be a little too tricky ... so I'd rather be up-front about the topic on my mind. Do you mind?"

Lucy looked back at the 3x5 card and answered, "That was a pretty good question. Are your other ones as good?"

"Maybe better," the son answered.

After a ten-second pause, his mother broke the silence with a loving wink at her son. "This could be fun," Lucy agreed. They chitchatted a while, and then she motioned to the waiter and pantomimed a signature of the bill.

Given the template set by that first conversation, the next few dinners were slightly more comfortable. At Lombardo's, Culpepper's, the Wayfair Inn, and Marty's, the 3x5 cards headlined politics, religion, the United Nations (both were in favor), and the best movies of recent years (and why). Her favorites were *Gone With the Wind*, *Gigi*, and *South Pacific*. His faves were *Grapes of Wrath*, *Adam's Rib*, and *Judgment at Nuremberg*. In the long-lasting debate that night, Chaz admitted that any movie starring Spencer Tracy captivated him. "If I could turn into Spencer Tracy twenty years from now, it would be a blessing."

The next Thursday nights, they went to River City Grill, Mooki's Bar-B-Q, Abigail's Cookery, and Blueberry Hill. By now, both mom and son had a good sense of the give-and-take that these dinner conversations would take, and both had begun to look forward to them. They had heart-to-heart tête-à- têtes about racial divisions in this country, the future of the cities ("Is everyone moving to the suburbs?"), America's role in the world, and "Is art outdated?" (a premature discussion since Andy Warhol changed everything in the next thirteen years).

However, one of the biggest discussions of the summer came at the dinner at Baliban's, a hip restaurant in the emerging Central West End. Chaz opened the subject matter by placing a 3x5 card in the middle of the table. It had only three words: *Subject: Gender inequality.*

"Holy moley," Lucy laughed aloud to her son. "Are we going to be here for the next ten hours?" She then looked to the waiter. "Perhaps a bottle of Chardonnay?" she requested, anticipating a long conversation.

Over the course of the next four hours, the mother convinced her son that women are equal partners in raising a family. "And perhaps, dare I say so,"

Lucy advanced with some trepidation, "perhaps more than equal partners." After a glass of white wine, she expounded, "We change the diapers. We push you to school. We ask to see your homework. We share your successes. We are crushed by your failures. We are forever in your corner."

The give-and-take extended for another ninety minutes. Truth be told, it could have gone on for another three days. Chaz was honestly obsessed with his mother's role in raising him, but he was equally as impressed with her lack of resentment that it had fallen to her. By ten p.m., both mother and son had begun yawning. Finally, Chaz called it quits. Unlike the earlier turnabout, Chaz extended his hand to the waiter and pantomimed the signing of a bill as he called out, "Check please."

The next two dinners/assignations were significant for both parties. At Ruggeri's in the section of St. Louis called "The Hill," Chaz pulled out the chair for his mother and, once seated, placed the 3x5 card in the middle of the table. After a finger drumroll, he turned over the index card and watched his mother read the single word. It was the subject of novels and movies, and the one mystery that every young person (and older people too) wants answered. Chaz, in particular, had recently become preoccupied with the subject and wanted to know his mother's thoughts.

Lucy picked up the card and smiled. "Love?" she read. "It's a pretty broad topic. Care to limit it just a tad?"

"Yeah. How do you know?" Chaz asked.

After a few seconds, his mom just smiled and commented, "Wow, that's a doozy of a question." She then took a sip of her water and looked up to the ceiling for inspiration. "The honest answer is this. You don't know. Otherwise, every relationship would work out perfectly. It's not science. It's just instinct."

"Right, but some relationships definitely work out better than others," the son suggested. "Just luck?"

"No," Lucy answered. She then invited the waiter over to the table. She ordered some toasted ravioli and chicken Caesar salad. Chaz ordered the scampi and then, almost as an afterthought, asked the waiter to bring two glasses of Pinot Grigio.

The whole conversation was the kind that college students loved to debate in a coffeehouse, or a school quadrangle. However, it had been years since Lucy had actually addressed the subject. However, she was not rusty or reticent with her opinions. A few *bon mots*:

"I think part of the secret is that sacrifice is not viewed as burden. It's just what you want to do."

"Disagreements are OK. Otherwise, one begins to hold a grudge because you can't come clean."

"It doesn't have to be fifty-fifty … as long as it feels close to that without taking out a slide rule."

"My biggest advice though is to not completely lose yourself or be consumed by the other person." She then took out a paper napkin and drew a Venn diagram consisting of two intersecting circles. There were approximately similar areas on the left, the right, and the shared space in the center.

She resumed her theory. "Let's say that's you, and that's her," she said, pointing to the left and the right napkin drawings. She then pointed to the center. "And let's call that 'we.' If there's not enough on the left or the right … the right or the left will lose interest. Understand?"

Chaz chuckled and said he wanted to take notes.

"No, no, no … you already know it in your bones." The mother took a sip of her white wine and assessed her son's intentions. "But why do you raise this? Is it because you're wondering about Leah … whom I know you call at least a few times a week?"

"You don't listen to our conversations!?" Chaz reacted. The son had discussed the young woman from Chicago in some glowing terms. However, whenever Mom had asked if it was serious, he had responded "Maybe. Who knows?" and then clammed up.

"Of course I don't listen to your private telephone calls. But I know you care about this girl. Otherwise, you wouldn't call her so frequently. My last three pieces of advice: Don't rush it. As college students, neither one of you are completely free. You both have studies and degrees to pursue. No. 2: Call her tonight. Let her know you had a great conversation with your mother about the Leah-Chaz relationship. Nothing makes a young girl fall more in love with a guy than knowing that he is more than willing to bring her up to his mother. Leverage that. No. 3: Enjoy every minute, and don't overthink it."

In a rather Hollywoodesque gesture, Chaz blew a kiss to his mother.

"I like this game," Lucy coquettishly responded to her son. "What's next week? Don't tell me. Sex? Chances are, I will not be so forthcoming!"

"No, it might be more revealing and more enlightening than a discussion about that," the son responded. He then romantically circled the table to back her chair and escorted his mother out of the restaurant.

Later that night, he did call Leah—and, as his mother had predicted, it was a wonderful conversation.

Their last dinner/seminar of the summer was at Kemoll's—the launching pad for Chaz's acceptance into the Missouri University journalism school. In advance, the young man had anticipated that it might be their most difficult conversation, but also their most needed.

Without much ado, the son reached in his pocket and stole a glance at which side of the card he wished to first expose. "Are you up for this?" he asked his mom, who had come to enjoy her role as the expert on all things.

"Go for it," the mom encouraged her son.

He then placed the card on the center of the table. It read, "My history." He then flipped the card over and revealed the payoff: "My dad."

For a few excruciating seconds, Lucy Conner looked at the card, expelled a sad decades-long sigh, and nodded to her son. It had been the one subject they had always carefully avoided. Bromides like "he was a good man" and "it was a bad time" didn't begin to explain the pain of his father's suspected suicide during the Great Depression.

"Maybe we should order first because this will take a while," Mom said. In agreement, he took the initiative to order a bottle of white wine and chicken scarpariello. His mother ordered the osso buco despite its hour-long preparation time, since she knew this would not be an aerobic conversation.

Before his mother became even more uncomfortable, the good son wanted to reassure the one anchor in his life. "Mombo, you raised me. Without you, I would be nothing. However, I just want to know what happened. I want to know why my dad was never around. I want to know why it fell upon you to be the most amazing heroine of the family."

His mother managed a halfhearted smile and entered the conversation gingerly. "Your father was perhaps the most talented singer I ever met. He could sing with any ragtime band in the country. Raves! Standing ovations! He would gladly work eighty hours a week in the St. Louis clubs and the river cruises. He was handsome, and an amazing lover." Lucy almost caught her last word before it was uttered, since she thought it might suggest that their relationship was driven by sex. It was not. They actually had an artistic relationship, but let me put that in her own words.

"Louis Armstrong, Duke Ellington, and other luminaries wanted your father in their bands. He was that good!"

As she picked at her chicken dish, Lucy continued, "Your father loved me, and … at the time … envisioned that we would be together until we were in our eighties." She then reached toward her napkin and wiped away a tear, or at least an impending tear.

"However, he called it quits," Lucy admitted with some invective. "Consequently, I have tried my best to raise you to be strong … and rise above adversity."

"Tell me about the adversity," the son asked.

With some awkwardness and sadness, Lucy reflected on her former husband's specialty. "He could sing a grand song," she said with admiring praise. "But that was his one talent. Yep, it was an amazing talent. He was a newsworthy star. An awe-inspiring headliner. But, despite his ability to enchant people with song, he could not react to changing times."

"And so he killed himself … and gave up on me," Chaz asked. He tried to move it forward, despite the difficult question.

"It wasn't aimed at you. To be perfectly honest, your father was in such a personal tailspin at the time, I don't think he wasn't thinking about you … or me."

For the next twenty minutes or so, Chaz and his mother enjoyed the meal and chitchatted about the weather, the upcoming school year, and the Cardinals' win-loss record—anything but the 3x5 topic. Finally, as they were finishing with coffee, Lucy circled back to the subject. "I'll tell you this. Your dad would be very, very proud of all your achievements. I'm sure of that."

"You think so?"

"Absolutely. Now let's get out of here. I have a bunch of photos of your dad in a shoebox somewhere in my closet. If you want, I'll go over them with you back home."

Two hours later, the two of them were still perusing black-and-white photos that were now twenty years old. Most were smiling shots of the couple. A few featured his dad in front of an orchestra. A few even showed father and son on the porch, the backyard, in a park … wherever.

Around midnight, a satiated Chaz admitted that the emotional evening had taken its toll. After a yawn, he kissed his mother on the forehead and said, "Mom, I'm so thankful I've had you all these years. You're not just a mother, but also a father. And more than that, you are a best friend. I could not have gotten luckier than to have you in my life."

Lucy quietly smiled and waved good night to her son.

After a few hours of tossing and turning, the young man ventured back into the living room, where his found his mother sound asleep on the sofa, surrounded by photos. Rather than disturb her, he simply looked at the tableau for several minutes and locked it in his memory with fond, fond thoughts of the evening and forever.

CHAPTER 10

1949: The Windy City Launchpad

In his junior year, Chaz Conner was named the editor in chief of the *Columbia Missourian*. Given the prestige of the newspaper, it was definitely quite an honor. However, as a daily, it also promised to be quite a grind. The young man particularly liked to write … and the rigors of personnel, crushing deadlines, and inevitable publication snafus had every opportunity to rob him of that journalistic high.

The young editor in chief was determined to take measures to avoid being gobbled by minutiae. He appointed Mitch Kendall as his sports editor, Carol Young as his arts and leisure editor, Andy Mooney as his front-page and editorial head, and Gerry Leitzes as his advertising director. He had worked with all these individuals. They had voted for him as the editor in chief, and he had confidence in their abilities. He also had the tacit understanding that he could occasionally weigh in with an article, essay, or op-ed piece.

As he told his staff on a Monday morning meeting, "Don't worry. I don't intend to abuse this privilege. Maybe two or three times a year." His staff signaled a thumbs-up, and he continued with a chuckle, "Besides, I don't think you'd like working here if I turned into some corner-office, ledger- sheet grunt who has no passion for the craft of journalism. There'll be plenty of time for that when we enter the real world of big-city newspapers."

The staff instinctively knew the truth of that prediction. They realized that they all lived in an academically enhanced dreamworld, at least for the time being. They had unparalleled journalistic freedom, supported by Chaz and the J-school. In the back of their minds, they fully understood that once out of college, the unsubsidized business aspect of journalism would inevitably rise in importance.

"I intend to take advantage of our unique advantages," Chaz challenged his staff. "Here's an idea for starters. I want all our illustrious alumni to have the chance to editorialize in *The Columbian*. Put more explicitly, I want to invite them to write in a column I will call The Columbian Alumni Corner. Here's a partial list just to get us going:

1. George C. Scott—on what he learned about General Patton.
2. Tennessee Williams—on inspiration and writer's block.
3. Jim Lehrer—on daily deadlines.
4. Warren E. Hearnes—on whether government works.
5. John Mack Carter (the head of Hearst)—on the role of local newspapers.

Sensing some momentum, he then turned it back to his staff. "I would like each of you to come up with a half dozen names and topics that might hold our readers' interest ... or perhaps even win some awards.

"And that brings me to my next priority: I want the *Columbia Missourian* to be the most recognized, awarded, and quoted newspaper of our size in America. I am quite serious. I want us to win the National Pacemaker Award, which goes to the best college newspaper in America ... and perhaps even a Pulitzer Prize. Let's think big.

"We will all gain advantages from these accolades, and we may even become better journalists in the process," Chaz concluded his stem-winder to his staff, who spontaneously applauded.

To the editor in chief's surprise, he actually did enjoy some of the managerial aspects of the job. He was energized by this staff's weekly recommendations for hot topics, many of which were quite inventive and provocative. For example, Carol Young of Arts and Leisure proposed a major-roundup feature story on America's newest and most jarring short story, "The Lottery" by Shirley Jackson. She pitched an omnibus approach, with twenty reviews of the stoning story by students chosen at random ... supplemented by twenty other essays from Columbia, Missouri, townspeople —including carpenters, insurance salesmen, librarians, and PE teachers. Chaz immediately loved the idea and approved. The revelation of the feature story —the students thought it was a twisted, perverse tale. More townies and workers thought it was a "slightly exaggerated" portrayal of the winners and losers in society. Given Carol Young's summary of these findings, Chaz ultimately submitted it for a Pulitzer Prize.

Andy Mooney, his front-page editor, suggested that Chaz institute an "occasional" international perspective on the news. "Not much business upside," Mooney admitted, "but if we want to win a few awards, they might actually listen to some twenty-two-year-olds."

Quite surprisingly, Gerry Leitzes, his advertising director, actually came up with a complete new editorial section. "Call it Business," Leitze suggested. "We feature five or six success stories in our community. If that won't interest advertisers, I don't know what will."

Despite some enjoyment of his new managerial tasks, Chaz did miss the actual craft of writing after five months of Monday-morning staff meetings. His first foray into the arena was a rather inconsequential piece in the Art and Leisure section. It was a 700-word essay titled "Who Cares about the Emmys?"

It led with the fact that there would now be two million TV sets in America. (about 1/100 of US citizens). In the writer's own words: "However, the quality vs. the promise, at least so far, is vastly exaggerated. Major awards? *The Pantomime Quiz.* Wow! Holy cow! Other TV favorites? *The Goldbergs. The Lone Ranger. The Life of Riley. Arthur Godfrey and His Friends.* When this supposedly miraculous invention wants to contain news or anything of substance, perhaps I will listen and not 'tune out.'"

It was really just a rant, but it did reawaken his writing chops for a more serious, sarcastic, provocative piece called "What's So Bad About Apartheid?" In this 1,000-word essay, he tore into the South African movement that had just institutionally codified prejudice against blacks.

In his editorial, he asked, "What kind of backward country would isolate people because of their race? What kind of nation would train them to only be servants? What kind of place would separate blacks and whites in public spaces? Is it called South Africa? Or is it also called the United States of America?"

He then went on to decry the segregation in the US military, the sanctioning of "white only" jobs, the ban on interracial marriage, and the police state that was required to enforce such social strictures. "It's easy to point our finger at 'those ignorant Africans' who are dragging their feet to join the modern world. Perhaps, instead, we should look at the mirror and point the finger at ourselves."

He concluded the editorial with salutes to the visionaries who crusaded for equal rights, including a little known hero called Nelson Mandela. "These are the men with courage. These are the saints. These are the ones we must follow."

The apartheid op-ed by Chaz Conner gained a lot of attention. It prompted letters to the editor at the *Columbia Missourian*. One rather searing critique, written by a certain Willie Gant, was directly critical of the writer: "Hey, Mr. Smarty Pants, how many blacks do you have on staff?" Conner's published response: "Not enough. Would you like to apply? I will be in my office at 9:00 a.m. Monday."

While it was not a premeditated setup; Chaz, in his later years, admitted that he had anticipated and even hoped for some turnout on Monday morning. He did not figure on twenty-two African-Americans who stood patiently in a line outside his office. The blossoming cameras of television news captured the event for St. Louis, Kansas City, and Chicago news stations. The still pictures, captured by *Missouri Columbian* photojournalists, gained exposure in more than a dozen newspapers and news magazines—including *Time, Newsweek, Look, Life,* and *U.S. News and World Report.*

As a result of these interviews, Chaz Conner did hire Willie Gant as the director of a newly created section of *The Columbian* called In the Neighborhood. It celebrated all the ins and outs of life in the growing inner city of Columbia, Missouri. The editor in chief also hired Sylvia Robbins as an associate ad director and Mikela Johnson as a sports reporter, with the special assignment to cover women's competitive sports at Mizzou. Just to add icing to the cake, Chaz did write personal recommendation letters for the other nineteen applicants on behalf of their journalistic ambition … should they ever choose to pursue that path.

The headlines for this generous act garnered many headlines across the nation. However, it paled in comparison to the actual reprints of Chaz Conner's actual article. The essay was widely circulated and debated in such august dailies as the *St. Louis Globe-Democrat, The New York Times,* the *Detroit Free Press,* and the *Chicago Tribune.*

The nicest and most unexpected accolade came from Bart Grimes, the Pulitzer Prize–winning editorial writer for the *Chicago Tribune.* For Chaz, the entreaty was compelling: "I was impressed. Compared to most college essays, this one has depth, facts, and emotion. Sometime, I would like to meet you if you are ever in Chicago. We always need good people at the *Trib.* Keep in touch, Bart."

Chaz, of course, did so with every opportunity. Before the term "networking" became vogue, the young editor in chief seemed to know the value. His thank-you was an automatic correspondence, but there were others. When Chaz determined that he would need to supplement six hours of college credits during the summer, he asked Bart which classes were most useful to a big-time newspaper like the *Trib.* Answers: feature writing and writing on a deadline. When *The Missouri Columbian* was awarded the National Pacemaker Award, he dashed off a note to Bart and told him how humbled he was that the newspaper had been recognized.

This award was quite an honor for the entire staff, and the J-school decided it was a good time to celebrate the hardworking staff with a congratulatory party. In recognition of the fact that staff members wanted to invite dates, family members, and friends, the university decided to go all out. They scheduled it for April 15 at the Tiger Hotel, just a five-minute walk from campus.

Chaz's girlfriend, Leah Carmichael, was so proud of her beau, she wanted to turn this into a "family" event. "Do you think it would be OK to invite my mother and father to this thing?" she asked innocently. "It would be a nice way for them to meet you ... and it might make for a fun weekend."

"I like that idea," Chaz agreed and gave her a big hug. It had been a good year for the two of them, despite a breakneck junior-year schedule. The daily demands of a newspaper added to the pressure and might have broken weaker couples. However, theirs was an easy, fun relationship; and the two of them really did value their time together—despite the fact that sometimes it would come at ten o'clock at night.

"Your mother has to come," Leah added.

"Of course, she does," Chaz agreed.

That night, he called her and arranged bus tickets and hotel reservations for her weekend. Lucy had already expressed her disappointment to her son that he would have to stay in Columbia during the summer to gain some college credits.

"Mom, I can't work thirty-five to forty hours a week running a newspaper and take fifteen credit hours. It's impossible! But this will help demonstrate to you that it's all worthwhile. Leah will be there. So will her mom and dad. And I'm supposed to give a speech. You gotta be there."

"Can't wait," his mother responded.

On the night of the award presentation, Dr. Herman Davidson, the head of the Missouri School of Journalism, presented the plaque along with a recitation of the criteria. He then introduced the editor in chief to accept the honor with a few obligatory clicks of the news cameras.

Chaz acknowledged all his department heads and every individual on the staff, including the secretaries. He also thanked the department for their support. "However, my greatest thanks goes to that lovely woman at my table. Mom, would you please stand up? Her name is Lucy Conner, and she raised me from scratch ... through thick and thin ... and always said 'do something great with your mind.' When I joined the army, she even gave me a reminder, which I carry with me every day. It's a Waterman pen, bought through weekly savings when we had none. And she said 'Write. Write. Write. You have it in you.' Everybody on staff has it in them ... and that's why we won this prestigious award. I would like to congratulate our entire staff and my mother. You are the best in the business."

Yep, it got a standing ovation.

That evening, a few serendipitous things happened.

Mr. and Mrs. Carmichael came up to Chaz and shook his hand like longtime neighbors. "I've heard a million speeches at these honorific dinners, but that's as good as it gets," Lou Carmichael said.

"I like the fact that you saluted your mother," Mrs. Carmichael said.

"Exactly," Mr. Carmichael added, as if it was his idea.

"And let's have dinner with your mom tomorrow," Mrs. Carmichael suggested.

"Exactly," Lou again agreed.

Fifteen minutes later, Leah and Chaz stood before Lucy Conner.

Leah introduced herself. "My name is Leah Carmichael. I know your son, but not as well or as wonderfully as you know him."

Somewhat speechless at this emotional intro, Lucy leaned into Leah and gave her one of those French "on-both-cheeks" salutations that look so affected today, but not in the late forties.

The young woman then continued, "I have heard a million wonderful things about you. And I so look forward to knowing you better."

Lucy almost cried; however, as she had "steeled" herself from the Great Depression and all the slings and arrows of the next decade, this was not the time to weep.. By contrast, this felt like New Year's Eve. Time marches on— sometimes in a grudgingly forward direction.

Ten minutes later, she found a quiet moment with her son. "I approve," the mother said. "She's a wonderful young woman."

Chaz then listened to the band, which was playing "Sunrise Serenade." The two of them danced as if they were pros.

Two days later, Chaz did send his speech to Bart Grimes of the *Chicago Tribune.* "Here are my remarks at the National Pacemaker Awards Celebration here at Mizzou. Thanks for all your support in gaining this honor."

CHAPTER 11

1952: It's A Toddlin' Town

For Chaz Conner, Chicago was a blur of big-city excitement, ambition, and romance.

The position he landed at the *Chicago Tribune* was a perfect fit for the young Missouri grad. Like all rookies on the staff, he had to do his share of city council meetings and local politics. But as his mentor, Bart Grimes, told him when he was hired, "Chicago is a big, burly, tough city … and there's always an underbelly of shit going on. Just keep your eyes and ears open, and you'll find some scoops. Besides, I may even ask you to write an op-ed piece or two as time goes by."

For the first year after college, the young man kept his nose to the grindstone and uncovered a few stories on police corruption and sweetheart deals for Mayor Daley's council members; but for the most part, it was straight reporting—always on deadline and impeccably crafted.

This was a good time to have a straight-ahead, regular-hours job. The reason? It allowed him more time to enjoy Leah Carmichael. By now, they had gone together for three years, and while one might think the newness would grow stale, it hadn't seemed to for either one of them.

Leah had gained an entry-level job as a high school counselor at the Latin School. It was and continues to be a prestigious, upper-crust private institution in the Lincoln Park area. As a dual psychology/education grad who practically looked like a high school senior, the job was almost automatic for the administration. In addition, her father, Lou Carmichael, had pulled a few strings.

Lou was the managing director of the Merchandise Mart in downtown Chicago, which was the biggest trade showplace in America; it sprawled two city blocks along the Chicago River. The place was twenty-five stories high and housed retail shops, boutiques, radio and television stations, ten floors of office space, and eleven floors of permanent showrooms. At the time, it was owned by Joseph P. Kennedy, who had evidently decided to sire a string of US presidents.

"I think she would be an excellent candidate for this job," Lou Carmichael attached to her résumé. In addition, an autograph from Joseph P. Kennedy simply added, "I agree." Who knows whether or not Leah would have gained the job on her own? She probably had all the qualifications to do so, but given Dad's (and Joe Kennedy's) interjection, we may never know; and that's the unintentional "damage" that could be attached to many young women's self-esteem at the time. True, contacts count, but if it feels as if Daddy is pulling the strings, then it can translate as legacy privilege.

Despite that conundrum, Leah did an amazing job steering young kids away from trouble at the Latin School. Yes, most of these teenagers were on a good glide path anyway—but as every parent knows, anything can happen. Anything can go haywire, and Leah seemed to have very good antennae for adolescent advice and course corrections.

At least a few times a week, Leah and Chaz would go to Rush Street for the music and the nightlife. It was always fun, especially when they could mix it up with friends from college, the neighborhood, or from their workplaces.

In addition, the couple did have a brunch at least once every few weeks with her parents. Chaz actually grew very fond of these folks, and he was quite comfortable with Mrs. Carmichael's wit and political views, which matched his liberal slant.

After about eight months of eggs Benedicts, it was only natural that he called Mr. Carmichael aside for an important chat. It happened at the Ambassador East Hotel on the Gold Coast of Chicago. At the time, Chaz asked Mr. Carmichael if the two of them could break away from the women and have a private chat in the Pump Room Bar.

The young man did not beat around the bush. "I hope you know that I think the world of your daughter. I also have such good feelings about you and Mrs. Carmichael, but that's not the point right now. This is about Leah … and, hopefully, me. I would like to ask your permission to marry her."

He paused and waited for a response. Rather than allow too much time to pass, he filled the air. "I fully believe I will be a good provider, but I actually believe it is more important with two professionals to capture each other other's attention and interest for a lifetime. She does. She makes me smile. I believe I do the same for her."

"Stop!" Mr. Carmichael said. "Quit selling! I already consider you part of the family, and this just formalizes it." He then looked to the bartender and asked him to decant a chilled bottle of Moët & Chandon. "And four champagne flutes," the dad added. "By the way, will this announcement come as a total surprise to my dear daughter, who has already hinted to her mother that you and she will most likely get married someday?"

Appreciating Mr. Carmichael's sense of irony, Chaz admitted that Leah would most likely not be shocked at the news and the upcoming toast.

With a good sense of the dramatic, Mr. Carmichael silently poured the four glasses. He looked at his wife and his daughter, and then at Chaz, and held up his flute. "To our new expanded family. Welcome." Spontaneously, Leah and her mother danced around the table … with kisses all around. Everyone acted as if they didn't expect the surprise news. However, it did not diminish the joy of the announcement in any way.

Given Mr. and Mrs. Carmichael's standing in the city, the wedding promised to be the blockbuster of the year. It was booked for April 25 at St. Clement's Church, a grand Byzantine landmark in Lincoln Park. The rehearsal dinner was scheduled at the Whitehall. The reception for three hundred people was to be at the Drake Hotel along Lakeshore Boulevard. In the months ahead, the invitation list would be a subject of much debate in the

Carmichael family. Should Mayor Daley be invited? Of course. Joseph P. Kennedy? No question. Studs Terkel? Yeah, let's do it. Jack Kennedy? Wouldn't he be too busy? Ernie Banks? Why not? And so on and so forth.

Months before that, Chicago was the once-in-a-decade host of both the Democratic and the Republican conventions for the upcoming presidential elections. Strangely enough, there was not that much drama about either convention. Every Democrat in town wanted their state senator, Adlai Stevenson. Every Republican in the nation wanted the reluctant World War II hero Dwight David Eisenhower.

However, there was a debate in the editorial room of the *Chicago Tribune* in the fall of 1952. Chaz asked his mentor, Bart Grimes, if he could write an editorial on behalf of Eisenhower as a newspaper "endorsement." Instinctively, he knew it was a long shot, since Stevenson was the hometown hero in a Democratic state. Add to that the fact that Chaz Conner was raised as a liberal Democrat and was now part of the "Kennedy-Carmichael" Democratic family.

He confronted that backlash in the first line of his editorial titled "Why I Really Like Ike."

I know I shouldn't. Mom will never talk to me again. My father-in-law will disown me. My liberal friends will avoid me in the Rush Street hot spots. However, elections are not really popularity contests for the voters.

I saw this man lead in World War II. I saw friends lose their lives. I saw him do his best to rebuild Europe. I saw a humble man, who would act when asked to do so. He is not the most eloquent wordsmith like his Democratic opponent, but what does that matter? Really?

Think beyond the words in this sentence. Think beyond rhetoric. Think big. Think Eisenhower.

Surprisingly and impressively, there was an actual heated debate in the editorial room of the *Chicago Tribune*. Bart Grimes, the editorial chief who hired Chaz Conner and asked him to contribute, actually argued on behalf of the young man's reasoned essay. He lost the argument to the advertising staff and the publisher, who had deep ties to the United States Senate and Adlai Stevenson, in particular.

In July, the editorial called "Adlai's the One" was published in the *Chicago Tribune*. Chaz was neither surprised nor upset with the decision. As he told Leah that evening, "That's just business. Fact is, I might have made the same choice … but it was a damn well-written editorial."

The couple had plenty of logistics to iron out before their wedding. As Chaz had promised to his fiancée, he would leave most of the details to her and her mom. As these fine points unfolded—the color of the bridesmaid's dresses, the type of floral arrangements, the menu options—he was so happy he had made this promise.

Every single day, there seemed to be a new decision to be made. What type of tuxedos should the groomsmen have? What kind of bachelor party should there be? Should we go over Mom's and Dad's suggestions for invitees? Who should sit at whose table?

Fortunately, Mr. Carmichael made it relatively easy for Chaz. "Let the women decide, and have no opinion. There's plenty of time to put in your two cents' worth after you're married," he told Chaz one night over a scotch and water. Meanwhile, the two men could easily chuckle about Democratic politics and Chicago's undeserved moniker as "The Second City."

The more time that Mr. Carmichael spent with Chaz, the easier it was for him to give a glowing toast to the young man at their rehearsal dinner. "I would like to salute the newest addition to the Carmichael family by introducing Chaz's inspiration, his spirit, his soul, and his innate sense of honesty. Her name is Lucy Conner, and she is his mother. Lucy, would you please stand? As of tomorrow, you are officially part of this family … and hopefully, we are officially a part of the Conner family. Agree?"

Lucy stood and sent an air-kiss to Mr. Carmichael.

"Once I met this woman, I knew that her son would be perfect for my dear daughter, Leah," Mr. Carmichael continued. "I promise you, I could wax poetic about Leah, but those who have been at other dinners have already heard my raves." There was laughter from Mr. Carmichael's friends. "She's the best catch in the world

… and Chaz is the second smartest person in the world (other than her father) to have recognized that."

By sunrise, Leah and her mother were both up, bright-eyed and bushy-tailed.

Dad came down the stairs and poured himself a cup of coffee with a smidge of cream, a morning ritual every bit as ingrained as his seven-fifteen alarm clock. He then joined them at the table. In his deadpan style, he asked, "Is anything good happening today?"

Both women were, by now, used to his Jack Benny imitations.

"Oh, Dad," Leah said.

"We need to be at the church at ten fifteen," Mrs. Carmichael answered. "And I want you to look every bit as handsome as the day we married." She then walked around the table and kissed her husband on the lips.

Somewhat surprised at her expressive act, Mr. Carmichael looked first at his wife and simply said, "Wow." He then looked at his daughter. "Hopefully, thirty years from now, you will still be as affectionate and happy as your mom and I are this morning." With that, Mr. Carmichael then circled the table and kissed his wife on the lips.

Mrs. Carmichael then looked at her daughter and then at her husband. With perfect timing, she then repeated the caption, "Wow!"

Three hours later, at St. Clement's Church, Father James O'Malley made everyone feel welcomed, comfortable, and loved. He even acted as if he knew both Leah and Chaz personally from childhood, and celebrated their union together as if it were preordained by the Vatican.

The reception afterward at the Drake Hotel was *the* place to be for Chicago glitterati. Mayor Daley was there. Ernie Banks showed up. Adlai Stevenson, despite his defeat in the November election, also came. The senior staff of the *Chicago Tribune* attended, as did the faculty and staff of the Latin School. At a certain point, Joseph P. Kennedy entered the hall, along with the top guns of all the Merchandise Mart consigliere—the TV stations, the media conglomerates, and all the major retailers who operated out of that behemoth on the Chicago River.

When the bride and groom entered the festooned ballroom, Louis Armstrong was singing, "Chicago, Chicago … that toddlin' town. Chicago, Chicago … I'll show you around." On cue, there was a standing ovation for the new bride and groom who walked down the center aisle, as if they had both won the presidency of the United States.

Everything was stunning—pastel rose hues and lime-green tones, model- worthy men in morning coats walking the room with champagne bottles in hand, and a swirl of local celebrities wherever one would look.

After a few hours of chitchat and a sumptuous meal of beef Wellington, potatoes Anna, and side salad, Chaz Conner took the podium.

"First of all, let me thank all of you for coming here tonight and making this an evening to remember for the rest of our lives. I would like to pay special tribute to three people. One: A woman I am now so tickled to call Mrs. Charles Parker Conner. Most of you know her as Leah. I know her as wonderful. Kind. Loving. Sharing. A kindred spirit. Everything a young man could hope for as he hopes to build a new life in this great city.

"Two: I would like to celebrate and thank my new mother- and father-in- law. Mr. and Mrs. Lou Carmichael. I have grown to know both of them over the past few years, and I must say, they are the easiest people to like. Sometimes funny. Sometimes challenging. Always engaging and embracing. I have never once felt I was on 'an audition' with them. That's how good they are.

"Three: I would like to throw a bouquet to the woman who made it all possible for me. Many of you know her. Even Louis Armstrong knows her! Actually, he came up to me after one of his songs and asked, 'That's your mother? She once taught dance lessons in St. Louis when I was a struggling band member and your dad was wowing crowds. This woman knows how to dance! Can you keep up with her?'

"Mom, I don't know if I can … but Louis suggests that once upon a time, when I was only three or four years old, you knew how to cut the rug on this particular tune. I say we give it a try."

The young man then held out his hand to his mother, who joined him at the center of the dance floor. Louis Armstrong, with his always-gravelly voice, acknowledged the middle-aged woman on the parquet floor. As the band was doing the downbeat, Louis took the mike. "When I was a young man struggling for any recognition … and she was a young woman who danced better than anyone in America, we lit up the clubs in St. Louis, once upon a time. Young man, I only wish you can turn out as good as your dear mother."

Satchmo then began to sing:

> *Give me a kiss to build a dream on*
> *And my imagination will thrive upon that kiss.*
> *Sweetheart, I ask no more than this*
> *A kiss to build a dream on.*

At that point, Chaz could not resist giving his mother the sweetest hug and kiss of his lifetime. After bowing to his mom, he then moved to his new bride, and gave Leah a wonderful hug and kiss. But the most emotional moment of the evening was when he asked Louis Armstrong to perfom the song they had earlier discussed. In memory of younger days. Satchmo then did a solo trumpet version of "La Vie en Rose."

On this prompt, the son escorted his mother to the center of the ballroom. Almost as if it were rehearsed, Chaz sent a wink to his father-in-law, who escorted Leah to the same space. On cue, Mrs. Carmichael joined them on the floor, squired by Mr. Joseph P. Kennedy. Over the next few songs and the next several hours, everyone was dancing. Everyone was happy. Everyone was convinced that this euphoria should last forever.

CHAPTER 12

1953: Lew

Leah Conner was not one to greet her husband at the front door *Leave It to Beaver* style—with an apron, homemade cupcakes, and a big welcoming kiss and a hug. However, on this particular evening of January 8, 1953, she had seated herself by the front window to see when Chaz might be walking up the street.

When she saw him stroll up the six steps and walk through the big wooden door, she stood there and jumped in his arms. "Guess what?" she asked.

"You love me more today than yesterday?" he responded with some puzzlement in his voice.

"Especially more today than yesterday," she said. "'Cause guess what? We are pregnant!"

"Oh my god. Oh my god. Oh my god!" Chaz yelped, holding his wife. He suddenly gripped her more securely, as if he was holding the most fragile vase in the Louvre. "Sit down right here. Don't move. Be careful getting in the chair."

Bemused, Leah sat down on the sofa and held her husband's hands. "Can you believe it?" she asked with tears of happiness in her eyes.

"Did you go to the doctor today?" he responded.

"Yep, it's positive. And it's really, really early. My pediatrician tells me we should wait until the first trimester to tell anyone … including your mother and my mother and my father. Can we keep this secret?"

"I don't know."

"I don't know if I can either … but we're only talking about eight weeks. C'mon! Whadya say? We can have our own little secret for two months, don't you think?"

In so many ways, the next eight weeks were the most wonderful, private weeks of their pregnancy. Both Leah and Chaz had made a perfect pact to keep it to themselves. They would walk and hum to brunches every Sunday in Lincoln Park and, while the waitress would imagine that they were just another loving, unmarried, or recently married couple, the two of them would whisper aloud about life ahead for the Chaz Conner family.

"What if it's a girl? Will you take her to ballet class?"

"What if it's a boy? Will you take him to Chicago Cub games?"

In a clandestine, "aren't we special" way, both felt they held the national secret from the entire world. In a twisted scenario, it was akin the recent spy novel just published by Ian Fleming called *Casino Royale*. It extolled the way that life can and perhaps should be hush-hush and classified—and sometimes in a sexy way.

On the way back to their home, Leah often liked to tickle Chaz and giggle that those passersby, these neighbors, so many strangers don't know that "we are pregnant, nyah, nyah, nyah, nyah, nyah." It was, after all, their secret. Given their glee, they were each somewhat amazed and impressed that each had kept it to themselves. However, they did love each other all the more for that silent compact.

Of course, once inside the house, all bets were off. The two of them would pantomime a baby's food at the kitchen table, imagine a little one in the extra bedroom, and sometimes even visualize a swing in the backyard. In that respect, it was prescient for them to buy the house eight months ago at 563 West Arlington Place in the tony neighborhood of Lincoln Park.

Even before the pregnancy, it felt like the right time for Chaz and Leah Conner to put down roots. Her job as a high school guidance counselor and his as a news reporter for the *Chicago Tribune* seemed secure and perhaps even promised rosy futures. Add to that the fact that the GI Bill offered World War II vets, such as Chaz, very generous funding and favorable mortgage rates for first homes.

The place was not a mansion, but it did offer the couple generous space— enough room in the front for a few bushes, and even a small backyard that could accommodate a barbecue pit and a few lawn chairs. The place had eight rooms, including three bedrooms. One for them, one for Lucy Conner or college friends when they would visit, and one extra room that could be used for a study or who knows what.

At this point, both knew the purpose of this small bedroom, and they would sometimes walk into the space and imagine their young newborn in a crib.

"You'll probably miss this as a place to polish some of your writing," Leah admitted.

"We have other rooms." Chaz shrugged. "The dining room could work, or the kitchen. I could even convert part of the basement into a sanctuary for stories or your schoolwork. I say we cross that bridge when we come to it."

"We have months to figure that out," she agreed. "However, I do have an appointment with Dr. Meyer next week, just to make sure that the first trimester is going according to plan."

"Would you like me to join you?"

"There's no need," she answered. "It's routine. But assuming everything goes well, I imagine the good doctor will say it's safe to tell people."

For a few seconds, Chaz let the implications of that thought sink in. It would certainly mean a joyous phone call to his mother and celebrations with Mr. and Mrs. Carmichael. Most likely, Leah would tell her friends and the administrative staff at the Latin School. He would also share the confidence with his closest cohorts at the *Trib*. Inevitably, it would also mean the end of the zone of privacy that had been so enjoyable for so many weeks.

"Mom, guess what? You are going to be a grandmother!"

"Mom and Dad, are you seated? Are you ready to be grandparents?"

"Jenna, I have news!"

"Ben, my life is totally about to change."

"Carol, have you noticed how happy I have been looking? Or should I say 'glowing'?"

With as many telephone calls that went out, there were as many that came in.

"Congratulations from the Marshalls."

"Big news. Big hugs from your cousins in Northbrook."

"If you need anything—and I do mean anything—count on me. Carol."

"This is Carol again. Too soon ... I know. But I want to organize a baby shower for you when you feel the timing is right."

Partly as a refuge from this deluge, Chaz did bury himself in work. It was an easy time to do so, given all that was going on in Chicago. As his boss and mentor, Bart Grimes, had once explained, "You will never have to look far to find a story in America's most interesting city." During the summer, he was responsible for a series of exposés about graft on the Dan Ryan Expressway.

In July, he did a feature on a Chicago entrepreneur named Hugh Hefner, who had just launched a magazine called *Playboy*. It eschewed salacious details and instead concentrated on the accelerating fact that America was become a more sexually open country. On the heels of this, he did a feature story in July on the advent of color television and how it might change our viewing patterns, our entertainment vs. Hollywood, and our inexorable attraction to the "big box" in the center of the living room. Ironically, this story seemed to gain currency and letters to the editor.

"I hate the fact that my family spends an hour in front of the tube every night."

"At some point, will we quit reading? If so, we will become a nation of 'listeners and watchers.' Sadly, I think it's inevitable."

"Welcome to 1984. Color TV makes that transition 100 percent certain. At some point, I predict we will watch an assassination in true, living, vivid color."

For the next several months, Chaz and Leah prepared for their "bundle of joy." He completely redid the third bedroom with gender-neutral tulip wallpaper, a white crib, and a white dresser and bassinette. She did her shopping for a baby carriage and more than enough supplies for months. Everything seemed to be moving forward on schedule until August 17, 1953.

According to Dr. Meyer, Leah was a good three weeks from her delivery date. In anticipation of that targeted time, Chaz had volunteered for an exposé on the O'Hare Airport payola for choice retail spaces. He figured it would involve two weeks of research and two days of writing. In anticipation, Leah had just given notice at the Latin School and had gained approval for several months of maternity leave.

Neither one of them anticipated that she would break water at Marshall Field's shopping for diaper bags and crib bedding. As any woman who has ever had such a thing happen, it is both sudden and embarrassing. At the time, Leah was inspecting the inner pleats of a rather impressive diaper bag, when she felt an undeniable flow from her midsection that rushed down her leg.

"Omigod, omigod, omigod!" Leah screamed, omnisciently aware of what was happening. At first, it was just a small puddle; but within seconds, she was standing in a significant amount of water. Moreover, the chain of events that this triggered understandably began to concern Leah. *Wow, will I immediately go into contractions?!! Will I have a baby in the next four minutes?!! Will I need to name him/her Marshall Fields?!!*

Her salesperson—a middle-aged mother of three named Mrs. Sally Higbie —took immediate control of the situation, almost as if she were a trained flight attendant. Without hesitation, she brought an armchair to Leah and held the young woman's hand. "Honey, forget the diaper bag. You sit here. Within minutes, you will be on your way to Cook County Hospital." The salesperson then barked to her assistant to get a wheelchair on floor 7 and an ambulance at the front door.

Soon, there was a support staff around Sally. When the pregnant woman was wheeled to the elevator, the salesperson forcefully announced "Emergency! Emergency!" and pushed every shopper off the lift. She then escorted Leah to the front door, where there was a waiting ambulance.

For the first time in the past ten minutes, she smiled at Leah. "Honey, this is all going to turn out OK. You are going to have a beautiful baby, and you are never going to be happier in your life.

If you wish, I will do my best to reach your husband. What's his name? Where does he work? How can I reach him?"

She answered, "Chaz Conner. The *Chicago Tribune*. 382-1623."

As the ambulance drivers wheeled her into the vehicle, Leah asked one question out of gratitude. "And what's your name?"

"Sally in maternity. They know me. Good luck. Godspeed. I will do my best to reach your husband. Relax. Breathe. Breathe." As the back doors closed, the volume of her voice receded, and Leah Conner was rushed to Cook County Hospital.

True to her word, Sally called the *Chicago Tribune* three times in the next few hours. She also called Cook County Hospital to alert them that a woman named Mrs. Conner was in labor and on her way—and that her husband would most likely be shortly behind.

Unfortunately, the call to her husband's newspaper did not connect so smoothly. After several tries, Sally was able to contact the *Trib* and reach the general operator. Without any panic in her voice, she did communicate that Mr. Chaz Conner rush to the hospital to participate in the birth of his son or daughter. With several subsequent attempts to Chaz's secretary, she was only able to leave the same message.

When Chaz's assistant—a young woman named Liz Johansson—received the call, she immediately tried to reach her boss at home. No answer. She then tried him at his favorite restaurant. Again, no response. She checked his calendar and his upcoming deadlines. In some desperation, she called O'Hare Airport and asked that Mr. Chaz Conner be broadcasted and paged with the message that he must call either the *Trib* or Cook County Hospital on an emergency line.

To Liz's credit, she hovered over the telephone until seven in the evening.

Before her departure from the newspaper, she again left two more urgent calls at O'Hare Airport for Mr. Conner to rush to Cook County Hospital and participate in the birth of his firstborn child.

At 7:15 p.m., he heard his name broadcasted in Terminal D, where he was interviewing a hat salesman for his feature story on airport businesses that served the travelers. He had just interviewed the owners of a barber shop in the main concourse and discovered that a surprising amount of their customers enjoyed shaves, almost as a restorative regimen, especially given the notorious delays and the plethora of connecting flights at O'Hare.

At first, Chaz had not heard his name broadcasted. The second announcement definitely caught his attention. "Mr. Chaz Conner. Mr. Chaz Conner, please call number 234 on any available red phone in the terminal. Again, Mr. Chaz Conner, please call 234."

The reporter excused himself from the haberdasher interview and found the nearest available red phone. "This is Chaz Conner, answering your page."

The voice on the other end of the phone answered. "Your secretary has been desperately trying to reach you. Your wife is in labor at Cook County Hospital. I would hurry." Perhaps she could hear him say 'thank you,' but it would have been from a dangling phone as he immediately ran down the concourse to the taxi line. At rush hour, this was, of course, impossible. Instead, he found the first limo driver he could find and demanded that the tuxedoed man drive above the speed limit to Cook County Hospital.

When he arrived at 8:00 p.m., he quickly paid the driver and raced through the doors, demanding to know the floor of the maternity ward. By the time he exited the elevator and skidded to a stop at the front desk, he was out of breath.

"Leah! Leah! Leah Conner … is she still in labor?"

The receptionist paged through her notes and status statements for several minutes. She then smiled at the man. "She's out of delivery. Evidently, everything went well."

"Omigod. Thank God."

"She is now in room 513."

"Which way?"

He then raced down the hallways, while some nurses motioned for him to please slow down. After all, there were babies on this floor, and new mothers.

When he arrived at 513, he zoomed into the room and discovered a very peaceful wife and mother holding a newborn. She immediately smiled at her husband, who was by now in a crumble of sweat and frustration.

"Glad you could make it." She winked at him. "By the way, you look worse than I do."

"Well, it has been a nerve-racking trek, but I am sure nothing to compare with what you went through."

"Say hello to your son." Leah beamed and held up the newbie to his father. As he took the 6-pound, 8-ounce bundle into his hands, he never felt more overwhelmed. War did not compare. A grenade explosion on his right leg was minor. His father's suicide was surely a scar, but not as dramatic. His acceptance into Missouri University Journalism School paled in comparison.

This was big.

This was major.

This was lasting.

Within the next six hours, they named him Lewis Parker Conner. The "Lew," "Loo," "Lou," or "Lue" sound was a homonym to his mother, Lucy. It also referenced Leah's father, Louis, without making the little baby an official "junior."

The bigger deal was they just liked the name and the chance that this kid could carve out his own identity. For several years, he did.

CHAPTER 13

1956: Getting Beaten By The News

Ever since he was fifteen and joined his high school newspaper staff, Chaz Conner couldn't imagine a more exciting job than writing a story against a deadline and seeing it in print the next day, or perhaps in the large weekend edition. In his early days at the *Chicago Tribune*, he would sometimes stop at the newsstand down the street and pick up the morning paper, just so he could gain the early thrill of seeing the story in print with his byline. Sometimes, he would even scissor out the articles and send a copy to his mom as evidence of the fact that her dear son was making his mark in the world of journalism.

Perhaps his biggest kick was the "scoop." In the past six years, he was able to beat the competition with stories on government graft, police roundups of prostitution rings, the emerging gang wars on the South Side, and the Chicago renovation plans for the "Miracle Mile." As he had learned, all it took was a network of reliable contacts, legwork, and the ability to meet a deadline faster than the other newsmen in town. It was always more difficult to be the first with the story for national and international news. Part of the hurdle was the simple matter of time zones. A bigger part was the fact that local newsmen on the ground had an automatic geographic advantage.

However, the biggest factor was an emerging medium that promised unparalleled immediacy. It was called television.

For the past few years, Chaz had been fascinated by the phenomenon. In fact, as an early adopter, he had two TV sets in their

Lincoln Park home— one in the living room, one in the bedroom. For the most part, these large furniture pieces with small screens were a novelty … since in the early fifties, broadcasts were only about two hours a day. Most of that was goofy programming—a puppet show called *Kukla, Fran, and Ollie* and a game show called *The Price Is Right*. And there was a new thing called soap operas, pioneered by a serial called *As the World Turns*.

However, it didn't take long before five minutes of headlines would cut through the hash. Sometimes, it might be ten minutes. Mind you, there were no reporters on the streets at the time. No remotes. Just a news guy reading off a sheet of paper about what was happening in the city at 5:03 p.m. Lots of times, it amounted to traffic reports, weather warnings, and an occasional crash on the Dan Ryan Expressway.

At this point, TV news was simply an interruption in programming. However, Chaz did think it might amount to more in the years to come. What if someone wanted to do a news-only program? What if it got a permanent time slot? What if broadcast news simply was viewed as a different iteration of newspapers— with headlines, sports, business, op-eds? It didn't take too much imagination to forecast that this might change journalism for decades.

Once he felt an inkling of this cataclysmic shift, Chaz Conner did ask for a meeting with his boss and mentor, Bart Grimes. A dyed-in-the-wool, inveterate news guy and prequel of Ben Bradlee types, he pooh-poohed the emerging media. "It's a bunch of monkeys on talk shows. It will have no long-term bearing on the impact of journalism. Nothing will ever replace the morning newspaper under every commuter's arm and the power of in-depth feature stories. Don't worry about it. You are gonna be a newspaper star. I knew it from the first editorials you ever wrote. Don't waver. You should do this for the next sixty years and win tons of Pulitzer Prizes."

His father-in-law, the managing director of the massive Merchandise Mart and compadre of Joseph P. Kennedy, had a drastically different opinion. Admittedly, his real-estate empire was being consumed with broadcast.

As he told his son-in-law on one brunch, "You are tailor-made for this new medium … and make no mistake, it will become the biggest preoccupation in our lives."

He then leaned into the young man to share a business secret. "We are planning to become the world's first all-color TV station. That's a game changer. It will affect presidential elections from here on out. I will have David Sarnoff come to the Merchandise Mart to turn on the switch at WMAQ. Things are changing … by leaps and bounds. Forever. If you need more evidence, watch Ed Sullivan this weekend, when this new guy called Elvis Presley will mesmerize the entire nation with his shaking hips and surly looks. After you hear this, think of Rudy Vallee as the old-fart print medium."

When Chaz and Leah and little Lew watched Elvis the Pelvis on *The Ed Sullivan Show*, it was convincing evidence that the media landscape was indeed changing.

Further proof came at the Republican at the Democratic convention on August 13 to 17 in the International Amphitheatre on the South Side of Chicago. As expected, Adlai Stevenson was again nominated as the nominee on the first ballot. However, there were some surprises at this convention. The Illinois senator decided to inject some drama into the contest by opening up the vice-presidential sweepstakes. He left it open to a vote of delegates, and a newcomer named John F. Kennedy was almost swept into office. The veep sweepstake was nip and tuck for hours. However, a last-minute panic of delegates who opted for "favorite sons" threw the whole thing into a deadlock.

By 11:00 p.m., after working on the news report for a midnight deadline, Chaz Conner did file the 900-word report, but was "scooped" by the networks. Holding his copy of the *Chicago Tribune* on the train, he could not resist hearing passengers talking about the drama of last night's convention.

"Did you watch it?" one man asked.

"It was fascinating," another agreed.

"It's like watching the news unfolding, right before your eyes," a woman passenger opined.

The next evening, there was another deadlock, and more of a groundswell for the gavel-to-gavel coverage on television. Ultimately, the Dems resolved the thing late in the evening by nominating Estes Kefauver of Tennessee for the vice presidency. However, the Sturm und Drang of who would be veep was riveting for many people, particularly those with TV sets.

By the third morning, Chaz Conner had become convinced that the tide was turning in terms of news coverage.

The Republican Convention in San Francisco slightly ameliorated the sting of being scooped, but that was only because that particular gathering was an automatic slam dunk for Dwight Eisenhower. To no one's surprise, the general was nominated by acclimation. As Conner groused to himself over a brandy that night, he could have written and sent that article days ago. No need to attend.

The actual election held only slightly more drama. Everyone other than the citizens of Illinois knew that Eisenhower would be reelected. Actually, even the Chicago citizens, if submitted to a lie-detector test, would probably admit that it would be a Republican sweep.

On the heels of these televised conventions and the broadcasted election, two men were named cohosts of the *NBC Nightly News*. They were the ones who anchored both conventions, captured the imagination of the viewing audience, and catapulted the network into a leadership role. Perhaps you have heard of them: Chet Huntley and David Brinkley.

The next morning, Chaz called his father-in-law, Lou Carmichael, and asked for a lunch meeting.

"You mentioned David Sarnoff once," the attractive young newsman said.

"You suggested that he might be looking for a fresh face for broadcast news."

"I remember the conversation," Lou Carmichael answered.

"I might be interested," Chaz answered. "Should we have lunch at the Merchandise Mart tomorrow?"

"At 12:00 noon. Flannery's, on the first floor. We'll put our heads together and figure out a plan of action."

CHAPTER 14

1958: One On One

To Bart Grimes, the chief editorial writer of the *Chicago Tribune*, it smacked of betrayal.

His prime protégé—a young man named Chaz Conner whom he had admired and personally hired since his days as editor in chief of *The Missouri Columbian*—had been seduced by the bright klieg lights of broadcast news. In retrospect, it was not surprising. The young man had looks, talent, charisma, and more than enough ambition.

The proposition unfolded in a rather ungainly way. The young man had proposed a "career consultation" meeting with Mr. Grimes. At the appointed hour, the young man sprang a "sneak attack." He asked his boss to patiently try to follow this journalistic trail. "I met with David Sarnoff two days ago at the Merchandise Mart," the rising star announced. "He liked my audition and wants to hire me for a weekend newsmagazine position. However, I told him that it would only happen on one condition ... only if I could hold on to a diminished, but important, role at the *Tribune*."

"Let's slow down," Bart advised. "Are you quitting?"

"No." The young man smiled. "I would like to hold down two jobs. A once- a-week editorial for the *Trib* and a weekend anchor job at WMAQ."

Sensing he had caught his boss off-guard, Chaz held up his finger and asked to explain the advantages. "If need be, I will leave tomorrow to begin employment in the broadcast media. However,

I still love the *Trib.* I still love the written word. And believe you me, I will bring credit to this august publication."

"I am listening," Bart Grimes skeptically responded.

"I have a hunch this can be very good for the newspaper in terms of 'a draw.' It's not like I will be a celebrity, but if the TV show is a success, it will increase the popularity of any column I would write … even if it's only on a once-a-week basis. I believe I could do such a thing for magazines, but I would rather do it for the *Tribune*—partly because I love this place, and partly because you are the best boss a guy could ever have.

"On the other hand, I know you are a purist. If in your heart of hearts, you think this is mixing oil and water, and you must have only 100-percent dedicated print journalists, I can certainly respect that. I'll be sad, but—"

"Let me think about it," Bart Grimes interrupted him. "My first instinct is, I don't like it. I love ink on my fingers, and the whirr of printing presses late at night. I love the smell of Camel cigarettes in the newsroom ashtrays. But I don't live in an igloo. I know the world is changing." He then lit up a cigarette and looked across his desk at his protégé. "You're one of the best writers I have on staff. I would hate to lose you. I just don't know if what you're proposing would have enough of an impact on our paper."

"We could try it out," Chaz volunteered.

"Let me think about it," Grimes repeated. He then pushed his desk chair back, stood, and shook hands with the young man. Privately, and perhaps even selfishly, Chaz Conner hoped it would not be the last time they decided to "shake on it."

Twenty-four hours later, the editor in chief contacted the writer. He immediately got to the point. "The management of the paper thinks this could work out well … and to both of our benefit. And I agree."

"I'm so happy to hear that," Conner honestly answered.

"We can kick around topics midweek, and make sure there is a column on Sunday's paper. It'll work."

"I'll make sure it does. And I'll make sure you will not regret it. Thank you.

Thank you. Thank you."

Meanwhile, there was much to iron out about his new program on WMAQ. In consultation with the general manager, Chaz had requested a one-hour, in- depth interview with one person on a Saturday or Sunday morning. His suggestion for a title, *One on One*, was greeted with a smile of admiration from a young man named Brad Philips, who was named the producer on this new WMAQ project. "Wow, what a great title! You're going to be a natural on air," the young producer gushed.

The two men set up a wish list of ideal Chicago guests— Studs Terkel, Mayor Daley, Mies van der Rohe, Ray Bradbury, Carl Sandberg, Ann Landers, Ray Croc, Frank Lloyd Wright, Sam Giancana, Bob Newhart, and Saul Bellow.

"You think they all need to be from Chicago?" Chaz innocently asked.

"Not necessarily," the producer answered. "Although it's probably a good place to start, since you are better known in Chicago. However, you can get plenty of people who come through Chicago. Hell, given your connections with the Merchandise Mart, you could probably start off the show with an interview of John F. Kennedy. You can't get a much bigger debut than that!"

"You think I could?"

"You might have to lean on your father-in-law for that, but I would think so. The senator and future president is not exactly camera-shy."

The launch date for the show was set for July 18, 1958. In many ways, the two-month preparation would give him time to become comfortable on the set and resolve his contretemps with the *Chicago Tribune*. Most importantly, it would give him time and space to actually attend the birth of his second child.

As a result of missing the labor and birth of Lew Conner, Chaz had vowed to his wife that that would never happen again. According to her pediatrician, this birth was to be around the week of July 4.

It happened right about on schedule. On July 5, Leah called her mother to watch over Lew, while she and her husband went to the Cook County Hospital. In this particular instance, there was not a sudden burst of water on the floor. There was no panicked traffic jam. There was no desperate paging of the father at O'Hare Airport. This time, she and her husband reached the maternity ward in relative calm, and he participated in the breathing, birthing, and miracle of their first daughter.

In contrast to the previous birth, it was relatively seamless. Consequently, they named her Serena. Of course, in the next twenty years, she would not be 100 percent serene; but at least at this precise moment, it was an amazing, calming, and yes—even serene—time.

By the time Chaz, Leah, and Serena Conner entered the house, the welcoming committee was ready and waiting. Mrs. Carmichael had her arms outstretched, ready to embrace the little one. "She looks like you, Leah!" the woman suggested. Mr. Carmichael was all handshakes and pats on the back. And Chaz picked up little Lew and hugged him tight so the new brother wouldn't feel like a second fiddle.

After lunch, little Lew watched his new favorite TV show— *Superman*. The women doted over the baby, while the men decided to share a cigar on the back porch.

"How's the show progressing? I've heard good things," Mr. Carmichael complimented Chaz.

"So far, so good." The younger man took a puff and looked out over the yard. "I think the show will have an interesting format. Good in-depth interviews. And, Lou, thanks for pulling some strings to get John F. Kennedy on as the first guest."

"He's a very personable guy. You'll like him."

"Do you know why he's in town?"

"No, but he comes in all the time. Probably fund-raising or lining up supporters for the upcoming election. It's rumored he's going to run."

"Well, I do plan to get into that with him."

"Maybe you'll get a scoop."

"I doubt that. These politicians are pretty coy this far out in front of a convention." Chaz then took another puff and chuckled. "But you can't blame a guy for trying."

CHAPTER 15

1958: 5-4-3-2 …

One hour prior to the taping, Chaz Conner met John F. Kennedy for the first time. He welcomed him to the set, showed him the greenroom, and made sure the man had a coffee and a telephone, just in case he needed to make some last-minute calls.

JFK then flashed a smile and said to Chaz, "My dad tells me I'm the first guinea pig here." The senator then winked at the interviewer and patted him on the knee. "I don't mind that, I like being first. Hell, I may even try to aim for a few other firsts in the next few years."

Chaz Conner was instantly impressed with the fact that this was a man of immense charm and confidence. He was even cocky enough to hint at the fact that he might soon become the youngest elected president and the first Catholic president.

"It will be a fun interview. And all joking aside, I am honored to be the first guest on your new show, which I am sure will have a long run."

Wow, the guy can switch from irony to sincerity in a matter of seconds, Chaz thought. *Well, as the man said, it might be a fun and interesting interview.*

As a courtesy, Chaz did give JFK some advance warning about the kind of questions he would most likely ask:

1. Your impressions of Chicago.
2. Why should you be president?
3. Will Catholicism be a hurdle?

4. What's the best and worst thing about being in the Senate?
5. What's the best and worst thing about being a Kennedy?
6. What concerns you most about America's standing in the world?

"All right, good topics," the senator answered. He then quipped, "I'll try to come up with some good answers … or at least try to reach someone on the phone who can come up with a good answer, so I can memorize them."

Again amazed at his quickness, Chaz then went on a limb and tried to match wits. "Anticipating that, that's why we made sure you had a room with a telephone."

The senator had a hearty laugh at the response. "You're good. This will be a good interview."

"Thirty-five minutes until showtime. Wish me luck," Chaz answered.

"And wish me luck," JFK responded.

When they were both seated in their swivel chairs, the musical theme began to swell, and the booth announcer said, "Welcome to *One on One.* The in- depth interview show that gets to the bottom, the top, and the in-betweens of today's issues. And here's your host, Chaz Conner."

"Good morning, ladies and gentlemen. I am very pleased to have one of the most compelling political figures in America with us today—Senator John F. Kennedy, who came within a whisker of being the Democratic nominee for vice president on the first ballot just two years ago. Senator Kennedy, welcome."

"Thank you, Chaz. Let me first congratulate you on your new program. As you might know, I love this town. I have deep ties here. And I believe this is a pivotal city and state in the future of this country … especially at this time in our history."

The young host knew that he wanted to kick off this premier show with a bang. A little urbane chitchat back and forth was not what he wanted, so he launched into the more direct questions. "Well, speaking of this time"—Chaz leaned toward the senator with a sly smile—"would you like to use this moment to announce that you are throwing your hat in the ring for the presidency of the United States?"

The senator did a slight double-take, but instantly corrected the reaction with some grace. "I'm thinking this is not the precise moment for such a momentous declaration."

"Why not? You love the city. You have deep ties here. And as you say, it's pivotal at this point in time." JFK just smiled, and then Chaz followed up, "I'm just saying that if you announced here and now, it would have the element of surprise."

Kennedy did have the perfect comeback. "That's for sure! I know it would surprise my beautiful wife." The senator then flashed that famous smile of his and got the interview back on kilter. "As I'm sure you can appreciate, a decision such as this ends up affecting everyone in the family. And I have a large family—brothers, sisters, in-laws, mother, father, and of course, Jackie and little Caroline. So there are a lot of considerations. And it's not all glamour. You know the nature of public service calls for sacrifice, and one needs to know if everyone is willing to sign up for that."

"Fair enough," Chaz answered, instinctively knowing there was no advantage in trying to ascertain whether little Caroline might enjoy a race for the presidency.

The rest of the interview was repartee. The two men actually seemed to enjoy the give-and-take. The senator was never at a loss for wit, but the young interviewer could more than hold his own. They discussed the Russian Sputnik, race relations, the importance of education, the changing role of women, and the need for the young people of this country to feel reinvigorated to America's promise. And of course, it would often veer back to the political landscape.

At one point toward the end of their hour, Chaz tried one more time to engage the senator on the upcoming presidential race.

"Care to handicap the Republican candidates?" the interviewer asked.

"Oh, I think it would be best to leave that decision to the august body of Republican power brokers," JFK quipped. "Of course, if history is any indicator, they tend to usually nominate the next person in line, so I wouldn't expect a lot of drama at the Republican convention here in Chicago."

"And that next person in line would be Richard Nixon. Would that be fun?"

After a second and a sly smile, JFK admitted, "That would be fun."

"Assuming you would be the nominee on the Democratic side?"

Aware of this trap, the senator did have to laugh aloud and good-naturedly wag his finger at Chaz Conner. "You are very clever. But that announcement is not going to come at this point in time."

"Fair enough," the interviewer avowed.

"Fair enough," JFK repeated.

"Senator Kennedy, thank you for joining us here in our inaugural program." "It was my pleasure," the senator said, and meant it.

The studio sound increased, the lights dimmed, and the two men rose from their chairs and shook hands. Almost immediately, Brad Philips pantomimed a thumbs-up gesture to the young host. On the heels of this, Lou Carmichael, Chaz's father-in-law and general manager of the Merchandise Mart, came out of the wings. "I couldn't resist, I just wanted to witness the interview in person. Chaz, nice job. Senator Kennedy, you are an amazing interview. You're like a rock star."

"I don't know about that, but I do think it was a damn interesting interview." The senator then ran his finger through his hair like a Hollywood movie star. "Lou, thanks for setting it up. It can only mean good things for this country."

Obviously, the two men knew each other; and despite a few traps, the senator had already calculated that this could only enhance his quest for the presidency.

"Well, I'm offering to take my son-in-law to a brunch at the Langham. If you would like to join us, Senator Kennedy, you are certainly invited."

"Yes, I might enjoy that. I think we might have quite a bit in common."

Over the brunch, the two men talked about their war experiences, their life as married men with young children, and their shared view that young people must assume a more engaged role in the future of this country. However, it was not an interview.

There was laughter. There was wine. There was brunch. There was also Lou, who would join in occasionally—but instinctively, he knew that these two men, born only a few years apart, might actually enjoy each other's company away from the TV studios of WMAQ.

JFK seemed to truly like the scene … and the waitresses who, one by one, fawned over him as if he were a true celebrity. After talking to one particularly shapely blonde, he did abruptly excuse himself from the table, explaining that he had a burning commitment that he must honor. As he walked away from the table, he generously reiterated that he had enjoyed meeting Chaz, and perhaps they could again connect.

"I'm not sure I'll debut my inauguration speech on your show." He smiled.

"But I think we can do business together beyond this interview. And as I said about Nixon, I think it would be fun. Perhaps for both of us." And then he disappeared.

The next morning, the broadcasts of the day captured the moment when JFK admitted that it would be fun to run against Nixon. A thousand miles away, both men smiled. It was a coup and a scoop for Chaz Conner's new program, which was repeated on many TV broadcasts. It was an accelerating dream and perhaps an unwitting prognostication for all of the senator's avid supporters.

CHAPTER 16

1963: Camelot Crushed

Chaz Conner and the newly elected president kept in contact, partly because both men seemed to enjoy each other's pace, political interests, and stage of life.

After his election, JFK, rather impulsively, asked Chaz to join his campaign team as PR liaison. Chaz immediately rejected the entreaty, mostly because of his ingrained Mizzou training that journalism is an honorable profession, and PR is a "commercial sellout." However, both men agreed to keep in touch and offer any intelligence that could be useful to either person in Washington DC or Chicago, Illinois.

On November 15, 1961, a year into JFK's presidency, Lou Carmichael knew that Joseph P. Kennedy was coming to his property—the Merchandise Mart—and offered to arrange a private one-hour interview for Chaz with the president's father. Through many previous encounters, it was widely known that the old man was not a "great interview." Yes, he was the ambassador to the UK and resistant to WWII. Yes, he had an unabashed three-year affair with Gloria Swanson at the Kennedy Compound in Hyannis. Yes, he made millions before the stock market crash, and then made millions more on the repeal of Prohibition. And yes, yes, yes … he was known to have contributed mightily to his son's campaign.

Rather than delve into the darker sides, Chaz structured the interview more on Joe's role in the election for JFK. Perhaps the best sound bite of the otherwise dry dialogue was an anecdote from the father regarding the nip and tuck, tightly contested election.

"According to a source of mine, you evidently asked Senator Kennedy, on the eve of the election, how many votes he would need to assure a victory," Conner asked.

After a sly smile, the generous patriarch joked, "There was no need to pay for a landslide."

The president enjoyed the quip and telephoned the interviewer that afternoon. "Nice job, Chaz. Thanks for not dredging up the Joe McCarthy and Gloria Swanson stuff. Any new interest in joining the New Frontier in Washington?"

"Nah, unless your dad wanted to pay for my entire family's landslide splash into our nation's capital."

"Touché," the president retorted.

Their next communiqué came from Chaz Conner in 1962. It was a package that included a letter and an album.

> Dear Mr. President,
>
> Last week, my wife, Leah, took a New York holiday and saw *Camelot*. I couldn't help but think it is an apt analogy for the kinds of things you are trying to achieve ... including many uphill battles. I encourage you and the First Lady to see the show. In the interim, enjoy this recording of the songs. Richard Burton, Julie Andrews, Roddy McDowell, and Robert Goulet are quite good.
>
> Your ever-reluctant but always thinking PR guy (but mostly a journalism guy),
>
> Chaz Conner

Evidently, the president often listened to the *Camelot* album late at night and enjoyed the last lyrics:

> *Don't let it be forgot*
> *That once there was a spot.*
> *For one brief shining moment*
> *That was known as Camelot.*

The journalist's next approach to the president was for a November meeting in Dallas; it was 1963.

"I think, given the upcoming election and the Southern resistance, it could be a groundbreaking interview," Chaz suggested.

Kennedy responded with a telegram:

> Given the circumstances, I simply cannot spare the hour, as I am being pulled, pillar-to-post, with all the officials and influentials of this big city in Texas. I need to charm this place that only marginally feels part of the USA. However, I have a better alternative for you: why not interview Jackie? She gets better ratings than I do … and it may actually help the cause of Camelot (which incidentally sounds great on the LP). I must see the show the next time I am in New York, and hope to see you and your wife in Chicago the next time I am in the Windy City. Hopefully, not in the full force of winter. Brrr. All the best, JFK.

Through a series of correspondences between Chaz Conner, the White House, and his NBC affiliate in Washington, Conner had firmed up the one- hour interview time at 5:00 p.m. on November 22, 1963, with all amenities one hour in advance for the First Lady—makeup, hair care, private telephone access, fax machines, and an outline of the subjects he might want to explore. With all the t's crossed and i's dotted, and all parties agreed to the boundaries of the conversation, it promised to be a wonderful interview about the bright future ahead for both the Kennedy family and America in general.

All that abruptly, gruesomely, and historically changed at 12:30 p.m. in the Dealey Plaza of Dallas.

With several hours before his interview, Chaz Conner had walked there from his nearby hotel just to get a sense of the Dallas crowd and the mix of reactions from Dallas residents. As he would later report, most of the crowd was pro-Kennedy. (Otherwise, why would they be there?) They were mostly families, many of whom waved small handheld versions of the American flag.

Despite an inborn, ethnocentric Texan bravado, there was a sense among many in the crowd that this was akin to a Hollywood opening. Perhaps because of the four-deep crowds that lined the streets, it felt like a big event. More like Mr. Gable than a politician. More like Audrey Hepburn than the First Lady. People jockeyed for position just to get a glimpse of the couple. Some pushed. Some shoved. Most just wanted a clear view.

Some moms, dads, and kids—unfortunately—saw it.

As the open Lincoln Continental convertible turned the corner, it revealed the very tanned president and the First Lady in pink, both of whom were waving with all the confidence of a sunny future.

And then there was that first mysterious sound that was mistaken for a firecracker. A few heads turned left or right, but most did not react. And then there was a volley of unmistakable gunfire. Worse yet, there was a head that exploded, his hands involuntarily gripping toward his neck—and his wife, in horror, trying to climb out of the back of the convertible. Within seconds, a secret service agent named Clint Hill jumped out of the trailing car and pushed the First Lady back into the vehicle. Within seconds, the bloody convertible raced toward the hospital. Within just a few more seconds, there was pandemonium in the crowd.

Chaz Conner took in the emotions, but instinctively, he knew there was a tragedy to be told—and a story to be reported. There was no chance to get a cab back to the NBC affiliate. Instead, he jogged to the NBC affiliate ten blocks away on Arlington Street and immediately demanded that the office supply him a camera, a voice crew, and an intern ("Any intern! Any intern!") to drive them to Parkland Hospital.

They arrived as the priest was headed into the emergency ward to give the president his last rites, and a caravan of official black government cars screeched into the hospital.

Within the hour, there were rumors that the forty-third president of the United States was already dead. There was talk that Lyndon Baines Johnson was headed toward *Air Force One* to assume the reins of the US government. By 1:53 p.m., Jackie Kennedy—with her tearstained face and bloodstained dress—exited Parkland Memorial Hospital in one of those black limos and followed a hearse to the airport.

By 2:00 p.m., Chaz Conner was on the air for NBC nationwide.

"I stand here before you at Parkland Hospital in Dallas and sadly report the most historical assassination in this country in over one hundred years. The president is dead. The First Lady is in tears. The entire nation is in a state of shock. And within days, the entire world will be mourning for the loss of this one charismatic leader who has, until minutes ago, been widely considered the shining star of the future.

"There is stunned silence all around me. Whispers and tears. Disbelief and despair. Thirty short minutes ago, there was a frantic state of panic, but with the pronouncement of President Kennedy's death—which, according to the hospital, was the result of a 'mortal wound'—the pavilion here went quiet.

"We will undoubtedly know more in the minutes to come, but for now, let us say a prayer for his widow, for his children … and for this nation."

As sometimes accidentally happens on these broadcasts, there was a backdrop tableau, which made the broadcast all the more poignant. Less than ten feet from Chaz, several sobbing nurses filled the background, hugging their coworkers and audibly crying just slightly off the microphone. It made every NBC broadcast that night, and even Chet Huntley came back from the remote report with a handkerchief on his cheek.

Rather than return back home to Lincoln Park, the *Chicago Tribune, NBC Nightly News,* and WMAQ's *One on One* asked Chaz Conner to gain any firsthand accounts of the mayhem in Dallas.

As anyone who ever lived through that time, it was a blur of activity and emotions. Schools closed. Foreign leaders threw bouquets of accolades. The FBI and the CIA were under question about how such a thing could happen. On none of these subjects, Chaz could comment being on the ground and at the scene of the crime.

However, the killer was still at large ... at least for a while. After shooting Officer J. D. Tippit, he was apprehended four blocks farther at the Texas Theatre. His name was Lee Harvey Oswald; and he was soon overwhelmed by a right, left, front, center, and back police force that took the man down despite the fact he was holding a gun.

That arrest was newsworthy, and Chaz did scoop that the alleged assassin did have some alliance with Russia. However, his biggest report came two days later from the basement of the Dallas police station. Through some contacts, Chaz knew the time and place of the prisoner transfer and had pulled every imaginable string to be in proximity. He got there early. From experience, he knew it would take about a ninety-minute wait to be in the front row, but Chaz wanted to see the murderer with his own eyes and perhaps ask a question.

In the midst of the prisoner transfer, the newsman extended his microphone into the battered man's face but was interrupted by a portly, middle-aged man with a gun who had a more immediate transaction.

Lee Oswald doubled over in pain. Chaz Conner immediately turned to his right in the midst of gunfire. Within milliseconds (but too late), the Texas penal officers pounced on the interceptor and smashed him to the ground. Within minutes, an ambulance was on the way to "save" Lee Harvey Oswald.

Twenty-two minutes later, Chaz Conner was on *NBC Nightly News* with a sudden bulletin. He had a bloody face (which he refused to have his production assistants wipe clean), and as he reported, he did reference the violence and the horror of the moment.

"The theater of the bizarre continues," he said. "Just a few minutes ago, the alleged assassin of the forty-third president of the United States was murdered in full sight of the Texas police force in their police station. I was standing perhaps two feet from the gunfire. Perhaps you can see the awful blood of anarchy on my face.

"The man jumped out of the crowd, and is reputed to be a man called Jack Ruby, who is alleged to own a major striptease club in Dallas. As of this time, we do not know his other connections.

Perhaps it is with Cuba or with the Soviet Union or with other connections within the United States.

"As of now, we only know that the man jumped out of the crowd and decided to kill a killer."

Chaz Conner, with some sense of the dramatic, did take out his pocket handkerchief to wipe off the blood on his right cheek. "We are now in an uncertain world," he admitted.

"However, we are now the most sympathetic nation on earth. The planet loved this president. The world abhorred a miscreant who would choose to murder him. And we are now confused by the order of law that would allow a striptease manager to kill him, point-blank, in front of those who are in charge of his safety. We have a lot to figure out, do we not?"

At Chaz's request, he asked for four to five seconds of silence after that question. He got it. For the next twenty years, it would categorize him as a thoughtful and perhaps even provocative editorializing journalist.

CHAPTER 17

1970: God Only Knows

On May 6, 1970, Chaz Conner published an editorial in the *Chicago Tribune* titled "Enough Is Enough." It excoriated the police action against the students of Kent State, who were demonstrating two days earlier against the never- ending Vietnam War. As a result of the confrontation, four college students were slain, sparking an outrage in many US cities.

In Conner's own words: "It's bad enough that we are killing tens of thousands of Vietnamese. But now, we have turned the bullets onto our own college students. At what point will we ask, 'What's the point?'"

Evidently, eighteen-year-old Lew Conner did not read that editorial. The journalist's son was not a particularly attuned newsie. Fact is, he was not a particularly attuned son, as both Chaz and Leah Conner had observed over the past several years.

School had always been a drag for the high school student. He could endure history and some literature classes, but the math and science courses were always a mystery to the young man. Mom and Dad tried to give him a tutor for these more challenging classes, but in Lew Conner's mind, that just made the drudgery more painful. Even his tutor had to shrug after a few months and admit that "Hey, if he doesn't do the work, there's very little I can do to help him." Consequently, he barely had a C average going into his last high school semester.

It was not the kind of academic record that could get him into any of the top universities, or even the midlevel colleges. At a certain point, both parents recognized this and began stressing trade schools or two-year community colleges so young Lew could "find" himself.

"What are you interested in?" Chaz Conner would often ask his son. "I mean, what do you see yourself doing four years from now?"

The kid's usual answer was "I don't know." When pressed, he might answer, "Working at some job."

"Such as?"

"I don't know."

This circular discussion went on for months. Finally, his mother broke the logjam. She sent for brochures at several of the junior colleges in the area and shared them with her husband. They offered courses in virtually every subject, including some that might actually lead to a job—such as sports training, criminal justice, and mechanical drafting.

That night, Mr. Conner vowed to have a heart-to-heart discussion with his son. After dinner, the dad told Lew that he wanted to get a better feel for the young man's future plans. "I want to watch *Hogan's Heroes* at seven o'clock," the young man answered; and Dad agreed they could have the discussion after what he frankly considered an idiotic sitcom.

When Lew came down to the dining room for the "What about the future?" meeting at seven thirty, his father had all the brochures spread on the table. He explained to Lew that he had his mother to thank for doing all this spadework, and that application deadlines were fast approaching.

"I think I've already made my decision," the young man announced.

"Wow, without even looking at the programs?"

"I am not interested in those programs. I want to join the army."

If this were a film and you could see Chaz Conner's reaction, it would look as if he had just been hit in the solar plexus by Muhammad Ali. Of all the alternative avenues for his young son, this was the one he least wanted to hear. Over the past several years, the newsman had interviewed countless government officials who seemed to change the boundaries of this endless war with every interview. He also wrote several feature stories about declining morale of the military men and women. Increasingly, coming back in one piece after a twelve-month tour of duty became the goal. And that was not an easy achievement. In the prior year, almost twelve thousand young soldiers had died in Vietnam. Already this year, six thousand had been killed. And for the survivors? Drug use, racial tensions, and insubordination were on the rise ... as was the abject rejection of those returning vets, who were often ridiculed (or worse) for their service.

In every way, it was not the soldiers' faults. Chaz squarely placed the blame on a broken foreign policy and an American machismo that refused to admit it was a stupid stalemate.

After his initial flinch, the father looked back at his son, who was still waiting for a response.

"No" was Chaz Conner's only verbal utterance.

"You know, I kinda thought that might be your reaction," the kid answered. "Hell, it might even be a way to figure out what's ahead for me. Who knows?

And besides, you fought for this country and didn't turn out so bad."

"It was a different time, and a different war," Chaz answered as he gathered the brochures from the dining room table. "I know too much about this insane conflict, and I love you too much ... so the answer is still no."

While the young man watched his father gather the community college propaganda, he threw one irrefutable rebuttal toward his father. "In two weeks, I will turn eighteen. At that time, this will be my decision. Not yours." The dad lowered his head in sad recognition of this reality and silently walked out of the room. For the first time in their long marriage, he slept on the couch rather than answer the uncomfortable question from Leah: "How did it go?"

Over the next ten days, Chaz and Leah Conner tried every gambit in the book to dissuade their son from facing bullets in Da Nang. Chaz fully understood that he did not have time to convince his son of the errant strategy of President Richard M. Nixon. True, he had promised a "secret plan" to win the war two years ago, but there was no progress on that front. Yes, the father could barrage his son with a boatload of statistics, but the young man was never good at math, so the figures would be like a torturous tutoring lesson.

Perhaps his mom had a better scheme. There was this new thing called the "draft lottery"—a perverse loser-takes-all gamble that would subject some with unlucky numbers to serve in the rice fields of Vietnam, while others could forever work on Wall Street. (At the time, it was actually televised, like the New York Lottery as announced by Yolanda Vega.)

This scheme was a response to a growing objection to the draft, which tended to exclude those from Greenwich, Connecticut (who could always get in the reserves as line cook or a barber) ... while assigning African- Americans from Biloxi, Mississippi, to the front lines. So, as a country, we decided to spin the wheel and assign everyone over eighteen to a number ... that could result in military foxholes and bullets in Hanoi.

Leah Conner tried to reason with her son. "You may as well wait for your number. Hey, for all we know, you may get a high number, become excluded ... and never have to serve."

After letting this sentence sink in, the young man responded without any invective, "I don't think you understand, Mom. I actually want to serve."

On his eighteenth birthday, Lewis Conner drove to the Selective Service office on Hempstead Avenue. He officially enlisted in the US Army and offered himself for twenty-four months of military service. He was quite impressed with the gratitude and honor that was bestowed upon him by the admitting officers. They saluted him. He saluted them. For the first time in a decade, he felt like a member of the elite. Just to add icing on the cake, his lottery number came up as number 38, so he would have undoubtedly been drafted—unless he gained a college deferment (which did not interest him in the least).

After basic training, the young man was assigned to a corps in Hanoi.

After six weeks in Vietnam, he was shot in the right temple; he died two days later.

After receiving the folded American flag four weeks later, Chaz went into his son's empty bedroom every night just to visualize the young man's life, touch the desk, and rub the dresser that Lew once occupied every day. Sometimes, he would look into his son's high school books, which never struck him as overly used. He led the father to summarize his emotions in an editorial for the *Chicago Tribune*.

The editorial was called "A Tribute to Lew."

It began this way:

I am not a fan of this war and tried to dissuade my son from fighting 8,000 miles from his comfortable home in Lincoln Park, Chicago, Illinois. However, he would not be deterred.

He volunteered to serve and die for our honor. And that's exactly what happened. Last month, my dear son, Private Lewis Conner, lost his life in Hanoi. He was not the only one to give the ultimate sacrifice that day. Within twenty-four hours, seven other soldiers were prematurely killed in their prime. I grieve for all of them, and for all of their parents. Like 33,000 American moms and dads and more than 100,000 Vietnamese parents, we will forever miss our son and his promise to this world.

Who knows what he might have become in his thirties or fifties or his sunset years? Perhaps he might have turned into an architect that could beautify our cities, or a chef that may have pleased our palates, or a plumber that could repair those burst pipes that bedevil most of us in the brutal Chicago winters. Perhaps he may have done none of the above but become an amazing grandfather of the next Nobel Prize winner.

Unfortunately, we will never see the results that might have been, or the impact that these young patriots might have eventually had on our world.

God only knows.

CHAPTER 18

1974: The Leap

It was a call out of nowhere.

Roone Arledge, the president of ABC News, had secured Chaz Conner's home number and telephoned his home in Lincoln Park at 9:00 a.m. The editorial contributor of the *Chicago Tribune* and the weekly host of WMAQ's *One on One* program answered the phone.

"Chaz Conner, please," the ABC executive asked, assuming there would be an entourage of connections he would need to endure.

"This is he," the journalist humbly answered.

"Wow, you sound like yourself."

"I usually do."

"This is Roone Arledge, the big muckety-muck of ABC News, and I am trying to shake up things here on West Fifty-Seventh Street of New York. I've watched your *One on One* videotapes and have a hunch you might enjoy the shake-up. It could be good for your career and for ABC."

After a few seconds, Chaz responded, "Is that your exact title: *muckety- muck*?"

Arledge could only laugh. "See, that's the quick wit I want on the news, especially the news interview shows. What do you say we get together next Wednesday in NY for lunch? My treat. Michael's on Fifty-Fourth Street. Are you game?"

"I'll be there at 1:30 p.m.," Chaz promised.

Throughout the next few days, he pondered the prospects of a new adventure. Truth be told, ever since his son was killed in Vietnam, he felt the need for a jump start in life. Add to that the fact that he had worked at the *Chicago Tribune* for fifteen years and hosted WMAQ's *One on One* Sunday show for the past ten. Occasionally, he had been wooed by other newspapers, magazines, and talk shows, but the particular opportunity or the timing never felt right. After discussing it with his wife, Leah, both reached the conclusion that nothing could be lost with a luncheon interview.

Also, it's extremely liberating to feel as if you don't really "need this job." It could go nowhere. It could go somewhere. Who cares?

It went better than Chaz Conner ever imagined. For one thing, Roone Arledge was raised in the chuck-and-jive sports world. Despite the fact that he wore a Paul Stuart suit, he exhibited mano a mano fist pumps. "Hey, how you doin'?" He was the originator of the *Wide World of Sports,* which was immortalized by Jim McKay's opening line, "The thrill of victory and the agony of defeat." For millions of Americans, it revolutionized what sports programming could be. Until then, it was basically baseball and football games. Roone expanded the portfolio to soccer, skiing, skeet shooting, weightlifting, fencing, ice skating, track and field, bobsledding … basically anything that pitted one side against the other.

In the process, he discovered that anything is interesting if it's presented in a compelling, dramatic way. As a result, the network expanded his duties to include the news division. His first few attempts had not panned out so well. He had started out with a program called *20/20*—but cast it with Hugh Downs, who tended to put people to sleep. He then revamped the perennial last place ABC News with three anchors: Frank Reynolds in Washington, Max Robinson in Chicago, and Peter Jennings. This flop taught him that viewers wanted one true anchor (like Jim McKay in *Wide World of Sports*). However, according to ABC research, viewers did like the increased pace of the news, and that was the impetus for this meeting with Chaz Conner.

"My name is Muckety-Muck … but you can call me Roone," the ABC president announced with a handshake when Chaz entered the restaurant.

"My name is Chaz," the newsman responded, "but you can call me Chaz."

Arledge laughed at the confident ease of the line, which he had learned to appreciate through the surprise and the spontaneity of sport. As he had already learned in his three-year tenure as news director, the "journalists" generally did not enjoy a joke on themselves.

After some obligatory chitchat about the Yankees, the Pittsburgh Steelers, the Boston Celtics, and the upcoming Olympics, Chaz Conner was actually the first person to probe the purpose of the meeting.

"If you want me to replace Jim McKay, I am not as good as him on luging competitions, cliff-diving, or pole vaulting."

Roone just smiled. "No, what I have in mind is a news program … but with the pace of *Wide World of Sports*. Unlike my mistake with *ABC Evening News*, I don't want many different anchors. I want one anchor—you. Yeah, sure there can be other reporters in the field. But one clever guy to pull it all together. Chaz Conner. And here's the angle. Given America's shrinking attention span, I don't want any segment to be longer than ten minutes. Boom! Boom! Boom! Some segments could be three minutes. Some could be eight minutes. But nothing should be longer than ten minutes."

Like a prizefighter, Roone Arledge explained his concept with boxing gestures. Every time he said "boom," he punched the air and smiled, as if it were a winning jab. Satisfied with his 1-2-3 punches, the CEO looked at Chaz for a reaction. "What do you think? You are the one guy for this. I have seen you vamp. I have seen you push for an answer. I have seen you get the quotable quotes in the morning reviews."

Satisfied with his windup, Roone Arledge looked at Chaz Conner for some reaction. "Interested?" he asked.

"Yes," Chaz instinctively answered.

"Great! I took the liberty of drawing up a contract," the cocky Arledge proffered and pantomimed a reach into his pocket.

"Not so fast," Chaz interrupted. "I said I am interested, but not completely sold. I have a wife who has a job in Chicago, and she is important to me. I have a daughter who is in her last year of high school. I have a job at the *Trib* that has been my mainstay of life for the past fifteen years. I have an audience at WMAQ every Sunday."

"All true. All considered," Roone Arledge countered. "What? Do you think I would ask you to give up your family for this job?"

"I don't know. This is the first time I have actually met you."

"Well, I wouldn't," Roone answered. "At least on a first lunch."

Both men decided it was time to change the subject, and they spoke about the mighty Chicago Bears, the rising New York Mets, and the first Olympic games in Germany since Hitler had rebuked Jesse Owens's triumphant 100- yard dash in 1936. Both men hoped that the upcoming 1972 Munich games would go better than the previous Germany-based Olympics.

Over crème brûlée and coffee, Chaz Conner and Roone Arledge retained a two-track conversation.

One was external: basic chitchat about the nature of the news business and the allure of New York, despite the crime rate and some very depressing— even dangerous—neighborhoods. The other dialogue was symbiotically internal on both men's parts. The unspoken summary could be captured in three words: "This is fun."

Roone Arledge instantly felt that Chaz Conner could catapult his network into the next several decades ... with some life and spontaneity. Chaz believed that he had could finally ally himself with not just a boss, but a down-to-earth compadre who might just have a vision for where TV must head in the days to come.

As they exited the restaurant and formally shook hands, Chaz did ask the CEO if that supposed contract was legit or just a ploy.

As a parry, Roone asked the newsman if he actually wanted to make news with his interviews.

Without a moment's hesitation, almost like a muscle reflex, Chaz Conner looked Roone in the eye and confessed, "In my case, it might possibly be just egotism, or just a desire to beat the competition to the headline—but I do crave a scoop. I always have."

At that point, there was a six-second pause.

Chaz continued, "I always will. I absolutely love writing. I absolutely love reporting. But more than all of that, I love being first with the story."

Over the next two months, the two men exchanged many telephone messages.

After raving about the lunch and sharing his enthusiasm with his wife, Leah, Chaz Conner did communicate with Roone about the possibility. "I've been thinking. It sounds interesting ... but would it be possible to base this out of Chicago?"

Roone's response: "It would be a little bit of a challenge, especially since I am something of a control freak ... but it's not impossible."

Chaz's response: "I don't think any particular news segment should be less than five minutes. I know you said it could be three minutes at our lunch. Too short for anything other than headline news."

Roone's response: "Agreed. How many news stories do you envision covering in sixty minutes?"

Chaz's response: "At least eight. I totally agree with the concept of fast news. My proposal? No story beyond ten minutes."

Roone: "I think it's time for another lunch in NYC."

Chaz: "You name the place."

Roone: "I like the influence of our first lunch at Michael's on Fifty-Fourth.

Perhaps that might be good luck for both of us."

Chaz: "Noon on Sunday?"

Over a long weekend with Leah at the Waldorf Astoria in Manhattan, Mr. and Mrs. Conner saw *Ain't Misbehavin'* on Broadway and enjoyed a steak dinner at Keene's on Forty-Fourth (thanks to ABC). On Saturday, Chaz enticed his wife to visit the New York Botanical Gardens (a rather obvious attempt to prove to her that New York was not all Subway graffiti).

On Sunday, there was an arranged brunch at Michael's on West Fifty- Fourth. It would be a foursome—Chaz and Leah Conner, Roone and Joan Arledge.

"I don't mind meeting the guy, but I don't want this to be an interview about me," Leah warned her husband before entering the restaurant.

"Honey, it will not turn out that way. This is just a chance to break some bread and get to know each other," Chaz reassured her. "If Roone decides to pitch a job right here in front of you and his wife, that will be a deal breaker, I promise you. He wouldn't do that. He's not that kind of guy."

When the Conners entered the restaurant, they saw Roone and Joan waiting for them at the bar. As soon as the ABC executive saw the couple approach, Roone got off his stool and approached Leah. "Wow, he's right," Roone said. "You are a beautiful woman. And this is beautiful Joan. Joan? Chaz. Leah, I am Roone." As is customary on these first meetings, everyone did handshakes and air-kisses.

And then Roone threw a serious curveball. "Chaz, I thought it might be good to discuss a contract before we sit down for appetizers." With excellent comic timing, he then broke his deadpan and laughed out loud. "I'm just kidding. I'm just kidding," he quickly added. He then looked in the direction of Mrs. Conner, "Leah, I promise you … if I were ever to try something like that, Joan would divorce me. She may want to anyway, but mixing business with pleasure is not a very good brunch idea."

Roone then clapped his hands together as a segue. "We are just here to have fun and make some new friends. That's it." He then escorted both women to the table and proved to be a perfect gentleman and Manhattan ambassador.

In the course of the brunch, everyone did have a few laughs. Without ever veering into interview territory, Roone Arledge did focus on Leah, almost as someone would do at a golf or tennis tournament/cocktail party—many of which Roone Arledge had attended. Joan Arledge, his wife of eighteen years, knew how to play the game, interjecting some clever comments without ever trying to overshadow her now famous husband. Chaz watched the whole tableau as though it were a Ping-Pong tournament, enjoying many moments and occasionally applauding the spectacular plays.

By 3:30 p.m., after several Bloody Marys, Roone insisted on his personal limo to take Chaz and Leah back to the hotel and to the airport so they could catch their 7:00 p.m. flight back to Chicago.

In contrast to the "air-kiss" greetings, there were now warm hugs from all participants of the brunch. As Serge, the limo driver, opened the door for the Conners outside the restaurant, Roone held up a "just one more thing" finger to Chaz before he got in the Lincoln Continental.

"Your wife is great. Please let her know that I had fun with the two of you. I will call you next week. We should talk about business. This was not the time or place. But someday soon, I hope it will be the time and place."

When Chaz got in the leather backseat of the limo, Leah had a hunch of the conversation.

"So, he wants to talk to you, but was smart enough not to do it here," she guessed.

"Yes."

"I must admit he does have a sense of spontaneity and a pretty good sense of humor. Believe you me, I was completely flummoxed by his desire to discuss a business contract with you within thirty seconds of meeting me … and completely won over when he revealed that it was just a joke."

After a pause, she admitted, "He's a little charming, like you. You are very similar beings."

"I like him," Chaz added.

"I can see why. Let it marinate a while, my dear. I really do not want a disruption in my life at this time … but I get the business chemistry."

Appreciative of his wife's wisdom and attitude, Chaz reached over and held her hand in the backseat of the limo. At this moment in time, he was thankful that he had been lucky enough to find someone so simpatico.

CHAPTER 19

1978: Balls In The Air

The Conner family had always been quite adept at juggling competing interests. For the past fifteen years, Leah had retained her job as a guidance counselor at the Latin School in Chicago, while volunteering on weekends at the Art Institute of Chicago. Her daughter, Serena, was an honor student at Adlai Stevenson High School in Lincoln Park, and was an all-state lacrosse player. Chaz Conner had worked for the *Chicago Tribune* for the past sixteen years and was the host of WMAQ's *One on One* program every Sunday morning..

On paper, it looked like the quintessential multitasking family (before *multitasking* was even a word). However, in the past twelve months, those balls began to be dropped ... and would sometimes even collide with each other.

Let's start with the most innocent. Serena wanted to get into a great college and make a name for herself in the big, wide world. Ask a seventeen-year-old what they want to become, and you will not get a straight answer. You shouldn't. She's only seventeen. Most college kids change their major in the first few years.

But unlike most, Serena did have a focus. Like her mother, she liked psychology. She was attracted to the study of motivation and stumbling blocks that could hold some people back. Like her father, she admired expression and interview techniques. She never saw herself as a journalist, but she did enjoy his weekly editorials in the *Trib*.

Not surprisingly, Dad had suggested she attend the University of Missouri. "Not for me," she immediately responded. Other alternatives suggested by Dad? University of Chicago. Columbia. Notre Dame. And from her mom? Northwestern University. Loyola. Columbia.

She was not a compromiser/appeaser student, and she visited all six universities with either her dad or her mom; but the fact that both parents suggested Columbia was somewhat persuasive. Also, she loved the fact that she could live and learn in Upper Manhattan. Given her grades, she listed Columbia as her first choice and was accepted on early admission.

As a kid born in the Midwest (albeit the biggest, most cosmopolitan, metropolitan city in the Midwest), it would certainly be an adjustment—but, ultimately, a happy transition.

Mom's dilemma was more bedeviling, but it will make more sense if I explain it after Dad's conflict first.

Chaz Conner was something of a media success in Chicago and throughout the Midwest (arguably across the nation). Every week, he made headlines; and on most of his Sunday talk shows, he created sound bites that were repeated on every TV channel.

Consequently, it was not surprising that Roone Arledge of ABC offered him a weekly TV interview show. Given his preference to remain in Chicago, he agreed to research the show from the Windy City and tape it in Manhattan every Sunday ... under the agreement that in twenty-four months, this could be reviewed with a permanent location in New York City.

The ugly side of this? He had to resign from the *Chicago Tribune*, which had become his first love of journalism. His initial boss and mentor, Bart Grimes, actually teared up on his final exit toward the door. As a result of his contract with ABC, Chaz was also contractually obligated to resign from his creation called *One on One.*

For the next four months, he would be off the air ... as he negotiated a new twice-a-week show on ABC called *What's Next?*

Roone Arledge suggested and loved the title of the show, since it implied a forward-thinking view of the news. It also required that after each story, Chaz would need to relate the implication of the story for someone. It could be the middle-class, the Republican Party, the Soviet Union, parents, military readiness, old age, etc. This particular feature gained some news value acceptance since it suggested consequences—something no other straight- reporting news program regularly did. Sometimes, it would veer toward partisan alignment, but Chaz was particularly careful to balance the consequences on both sides of the political aisle.

For example, Jimmy Carter gave a speech about "a malaise" among United States citizens." Chaz Conner answered, "What's next? What will come of calling Americans afflicted with malaise? Most likely, a patriotic uprising in the US electorate, which might favor someone like Ronald Reagan, or some other candidate who will repudiate malaise (which few American citizens even understand, or even know how to pronounce)."

That particular rebuttal captured instant news since it came only twenty- four hours after Carter's statement, and it was repeated on many cable news channels.

The quick pace of the show and Chaz Conner's personality made it a hit, especially among the commercially prized under-forty viewing audience. They tended to like the irreverent tone of the show and the stories, which occasionally dipped into pop culture.

Leah Conner's midlife transition was not as readily apparent to her. When her son, Lewis, had died in Vietnam, she admittedly went into a funk and felt she was spiraling down. Her daughter's decision to attend college in New York made her feel even more alone. And her husband Chaz's new national popularity and frequent trips to Manhattan just made her feel more isolated.

Her part-time volunteering at the Art Institute helped revive her spirits. What did she do there? Mostly fund-raising, but it did keep her connected with the glitterati of Chicago, especially at their gala fund-raisers, which were heavily attended by her Lincoln Park neighbors and the Gold Coast movers and shakers. However, in her heart, she knew this was just a satisfying avocation, not a life mission.

Her first intellectual love was psychology, but over the past decade, the routine of being a high school guidance counselor had begun to lose its allure. Year after year, she faced the same questions from students: "I don't feel popular enough." "I don't get along with my dad." "I hate my teacher" or "I think my teacher hates me." As she imagined years ago, she could just reach for a folder of answers to these typical questions and push it across the desk to the distressed student. The very idea of another decade of these same laments was, frankly, depressing.

There was no automatically evident path for Leah.

Chaz had often suggested that the two of them gain a fresh new start in Manhattan, especially since their daughter had now been accepted at Columbia University. "This is a no-brainer," he often said. "We both get a chance to reinvent our lives in the most exciting city on earth."

"No, my roots are here. My life is here. My friends are here," she would normally push back. "That may be good for you and Serena, but not for me."

Flummoxed by her inflexibility, Chaz then tried to ascertain her midlife interests. "Well, let's just say that a genie came down right now at this dining room table and said, 'I'll grant you a wish. Tell me how you wish to spend the next fifteen years, and it will come true.' What would your answer be?"

"Chaz, that's a ridiculous game. And my life is not a goddamn game."

Chances are, you get the idea. There was tension in this marriage. Truth be told, it had probably reared its ugly head when Leah had spent a few too many years in the same job at the same school, and Chaz had felt reinvigorated with his new ABC job. But at this family crossroads, it was magnified.

Ultimately, Leah decided to explore getting a master's degree in psychology, with an orientation to art therapy. She sent out applications to the University of Chicago, Loyola on Lake Michigan, Notre Dame, and the University of Miami. When Chaz saw some of the brochures come into the house, he was understandably curious.

"Why the University of Miami?" he asked.

"They have a great art therapy program," Leah snapped back.

"Yeah, but it's a tough commute, don't you think?"

"Well, if you're able to go to New York twice a week, why can't I go to Miami during that week?"

After letting this thought sink in, Chaz did his best to answer without anger.

"Because it will destroy our marriage."

"Such as it is," she immediately responded.

That night, they did not talk. They did not sleep in the same bed, but that practice had been in effect for the past few years. As a last-ditch effort, Chaz did his best persuade Leah to apply to NYU and Columbia University. As he told her one night, "We could all be in the same city. You, me, Serena. Fresh starts. Rebirth! Hey, maybe you and Serena could end up on the same campus!"

"Wow, do you really think I want to walk the same quadrangle and go to parties with my twenty-one-year-old daughter? You really don't know me."

After months of walking on eggshells, Leah finally brought up the idea of a trial separation. She had just been accepted into the master's program at Loyola and wanted to devote herself to this new pursuit. "Besides, you have a nonstop schedule that could probably be better achieved in New York without all those weekly commutes back home," she said to her husband. "It might be liberating for both of us at this point of our lives to chase our new passions."

After months of turmoil, Chaz felt he had run out of arguments. Instead, he simply and silently kissed his wife on the forehead and returned to his desk to resume his work.

Unfortunately, that's how these fairy-tale marriages sometimes end. Decades of happiness, and then poof! In retrospect, there were many telltale signs along way. But that's only in retrospect. Along the journey, a shorthand between couples fuzzes the sharp points and hazes the highs of a relationship. And then, in a blur of confusion, all either party can envision is life without the other.

That very night, Chaz called Roone Arledge at ABC and said that it might be advantageous to move to Manhattan. Without asking a single question—as he was in the midst of his own divorce—Roone instantly understood and agreed. "Given the momentum we now have, I think it will be a bonanza for the show, and for you. Tell me when you are coming in, and I will have a limo meet you. I will also vouch for a six-month apartment rental until you can figure out your next moves."

CHAPTER 20

1980: REBIRTH

After Chaz Conner's messy divorce from Leah, he opted for a restart of his life in the electric, nonstop life of New York City. As a forty-five-year-old transplant, it was challenging—but also quite exhilarating.

He settled on 155 East Thirty-Eighth Street in Murray Hill. It was a safe, but not glorious, neighborhood in Manhattan. However, it was convenient to everything. Within five minutes, he could be in Grand Central Station and catch the subway down to Gracie Mansion, or the UN building, or the Theater District.

The best part of the move was the impact of his job at ABC News. The show—called *What's Next?*—had become something of a media darling. Within eighteen months, it had become one of the top twenty shows, according to the Nielsen ratings.

Roone Arledge's promotion of the show also helped catapult its popularity. The commercial was a fast-paced sound-bite montage of Chaz Conner interviews.

The spot went like this.

It began with a severe, silent, straight-laced shot of Chaz Conner at a traditional news desk. Over this stern shot, an announcer speaks.

VO: "There is a new kind of news program on ABC."

As soon as the last word was uttered, the camera swish panned to the left and introduced the lettering "What's Next?"

It then revealed Chaz on an airport tarmac.

Chaz: "Braniff has gone bankrupt. Implication? Clever costumes do not make an airline."

Swish pan to Chaz wearing one white glove.

Chaz: "Michael Jackson's 'Thriller' is now the biggest album of all time. Will we all learn the moonwalk?"

Over an extended dancing view of the "What's Next?" title, the logo movement is evocative of Michael Jackson's moonwalk.

An announcer sets the premise of the commercial.

VO: "It's not some static, 'just the facts, ma'am' kind of journalism. It's fast. It's exciting. It communicates the consequences of the news stories."

The camera cuts to Chaz holding a Tylenol bottle on the streets of Chicago.

Chaz: "Seven people dead. Result? Thanks to Johnson and Johnson, you will find more tamper-proof packages."

Swish pan to Chaz at the Vietnam Memorial.

Chaz: "People died there, including my son. Question: Will it have been in vain?"

Swish pan to Chaz wearing earphones.

Chaz: "Sony has just introduced the first ever CD player. What's next? CDs?"

Swish pan to Chaz in front of a computer.

Chaz: "And *Time Magazine*'s man of the year? Not a man, not a woman, not a human! The computer! What does this mean? Are we more prone to communicate via electronics rather than personal communications?

Over the last five seconds of this commercial, the camera swish pans right and left at a dizzying pace, and finally settles on the logo.

An announcer sums up the spot.

VO: "What's next? Unless you tune in, you will never know."

The commercial won a CLIO Award in New York the next year for the best media commercial. Given the judging profile (twentysomething and metro based), it was the favorite to capture the trophy. To Chaz's and Roone's surprise, the commercial did generate agreeing, appreciative applause from the audience. Neither man climbed the stage to accept the award. This was an ad agency event, and the small agency—Dimassimo Goldstein—that created, edited, and produced the spot climbed the stairs and held the trophy over their heads as if it were an Oscar.

Afterward, Roone and Chaz privately celebrated the honor at the 21 Club. After comparing their failed marriages, both men inevitably launched into the discussion about the ever-evolving news business. They discussed the rumor that Tom Brokaw would soon replace David Brinkley on *NBC Nightly News.* Dan Rather had just assumed the job at CBS, after the venerable Walter Cronkite.

"He won't last," Roone predicted. "Too much fire and ire for the *Nightly News.*"

Roone then addressed his situation at ABC. A few years back, he had appointed a troika of newspeople to climb out of the basement of ratings.

Unfortunately, Frank Reynolds had recently died, and Max Robinson was not considered ready for the sole anchor chair. "What do you think?" Roone queried.

"Are you asking whether I am interested in job? I definitely am not. I am a little too freewheeling to be strapped in an anchor chair every evening."

"I agree," Roone said with a smile, happy that he wouldn't have to dissuade an ego from the evening news. "What do you think of Peter Jennings?"

"Never met him, but I like him ... and I don't think he is too aristocratic for an American audience. He just sounds like a bloke who is smart."

After motioning another round of drinks, Roone lit up a cigarette and saluted Chaz. "You are a smart man, and a huge asset to the network."

"And you, I believe, are a friend," Chaz responded, uncharacteristically revealing his true inner emotions.

"I feel the same way about you," Roone responded. "As a friend, I need to figure out a way to expand the franchise of *What's Next?* without diluting your national appeal."

"What do you mean?"

"I want to expand the program to twice a week. Wednesday prime time and Sunday."

"I don't know that I have enough hours in a week to do that."

"You don't. That's why I am proposing a different format for Wednesday."

Chaz received his vodka on the rocks and decided it was a good time to let this new information sink in. He took a sip and smiled at his boss. Roone gauged his star employee and smiled back. Despite the fact that he enjoyed gamesmanship, he did not wish to upset his most popular anchor.

"Chaz, don't panic. You will have full control of both programs," Roone reassured him. "Given the success of the show, it is bad business to not expand the franchise … and you must be the anchor of both shows. Otherwise, it is not a franchise."

"Good to hear," Chaz responded.

"However, two touring shows a week is too much to put on the shoulders of any one person. So we will need to build up a staff of correspondents who will report to you. You will divvy up the stories according to their particular talents. You will need editorial authority of anything that goes on the air. And more importantly, you will have the responsibility to comment on any of their reports with a '*What's next?*' response."

"Will I have the authority to hire the correspondents?" Chaz asked.

"Yes, but with a second interview by me. After all, it is my damn network."

"Twice a week. Twice the work," Chaz expressed with some exasperation.

"Twice the pay," Roone added before he could think twice.

"Deal!" Chaz responded and shook Roone's hand.

In the next four months, Chaz interviewed many possible correspondents. He instinctively knew he wanted a diverse, youth-oriented quartet. Ultimately, he recommended four nominees:

1. Jon Scott—He came via Chaz's Missouri J-school connections. Jon was young, enthusiastic, and athletic.
2. Kaity Tong—He met her at a media party in New York and liked her bright-eyed attitude and intellect. For days, he watched her delivery on local networks and appreciated her style.

3. Meredith Viera—The woman was a knockout and had East Coast pedigree, having come from Newport, Rhode Island. Also, she was a brain.
4. Star Jones—A large African-American woman who had some connections with Hollywood, and pop culture.

Upon watching the videotapes of the four possible correspondents, Roone immediately approved the quartet and congratulated Chaz for his foresight to represent the new face of America. Once it was all finalized, he promised a new commercial to introduce the new Wednesday time slot and feature the expanded journalistic cast of characters.

Thanks to his ad agency, it was just as engaging as the first award-winning spot. This one featured Chaz turning left and right as an implication that he was introducing his new cast of stellar journalists over the voice-over of *What's Next?* With each turn, live action of the correspondents would be featured with their names. At the end of the commercial, Chaz looked at the camera and asked, "Who's next?" A slow dissolve suggested the answer: "You."

Over the next few months, the Wednesday show gathered a sizable audience—not quite the numbers of the Sunday blockbuster, but still quite good.

Chaz's daughter, Serena, had been noticing the commercials and often ribbed her dad that he was turning into "Crazy Eddie"—the ubiquitous electronic spokesman on every New York TV channel.

"It's not that bad, is it?" her father asked.

"Not quite, but every time I turn on the tube, I see you."

"Yeah, well, let's see each other in person. How about dinner Wednesday night?"

"Great. I might want to bring a friend. His name is Tom."

"Wow, so I should maybe be on my best behavior?"

"That would be nice."

"Café des Artistes—8:00 p.m. Bring Tom.

"Bring your manners."

"Love you."

"Love you back."

Chaz reserved his favorite table at this landmark restaurant and got there twenty minutes early. To his dismay, he only saw his daughter every three weeks or so; but every time they got together, he was thrilled. Admittedly, she was quite busy with her course load, as was he with his twice-a-week program, but their get-togethers were always happy times.

Serena had decided to major in psychology, as her mother had done, and seemed to be quite happy with the curricula. "It's interesting to learn how people think and feel," she once told her dad.

"Yes, but for my taste, the bigger intrigue is how people act. For me, that's the nature of news," Chaz retorted.

"Yeah, but they act a certain way because they feel a certain way," Serena would often rebut—as did her mother, Leah.

Through decades of marriage, Chaz had learned not to challenge the psychobabble argument, as he liked to privately call it. The man was a more pragmatic soul. What people did mattered to him. The choices they made determined history. The actions they took created war and peace. It always mattered less to him how they felt about their decisions. Perhaps that's the difference between hard news and softer sciences, like psychology.

Despite that intellectual gap, father and daughter seemed to be absolutely simpatico and equally in love with their New York experiences. She often bragged about her dad and admired the fact that he kept himself in relatively good shape. Chaz believed that his daughter had turned into a very confident, beautiful young woman. But what of this guy called Tom?

Unlike any of his other brunch, dinner, or theater dates, this was the first time Serena wanted to introduce a "boyfriend." For a few seconds, Chaz thought that Tom was maybe just a buddy, not a main squeeze.

Of course not, he told himself. *He's a boyfriend who wants to introduce himself to Mr. Conner ... or perhaps Serena wants to introduce me to him. Either way, it's an audition.*

After mulling these thoughts over a Stoli on the rocks at the bar, the couple came into Café des Artistes.

Serena gave him an enthusiastic hug and kiss. Immediately softened by the affection, he honestly told her, "Oh my god, you get more beautiful every time I see you."

"And, Dad, this is my friend Tom Conley. We go to school together at Columbia. Different disciplines but similar interests."

After thirty years in the journalism business, Chaz was a veteran at meeting strangers and making them feel at ease. He extended his right hand to the young man, shook it firmly, and said, "Tom, I am very happy to meet you ... and look forward to getting to know you better. Let's do it over a delicious meal." He then extended his hand toward the dining room and escorted the couple to table like a maître d'.

As it turned out, it was a delightful dinner. For the first thirty minutes of the encounter, Tom asked Chaz every possible question about his new show:

"Do you love finding facts?"

"Who has been your favorite interview?"

"How much is ad-libbed?"

"Do you like the network?"

"How well do you get along with your correspondents?"

Like every human being, Chaz was susceptible to outward adoration. He had learned the technique early in his J-school training but had almost forgotten it, until young Tom Conley reminded him how good it felt to be admired.

"OK, let's change places," Chaz announced after a half hour. In a dramatic but funny gesture, the father scooted out of the bench seat and asked the young man to change sides and sit in his seat.

The barrage of questions began:

"What are you studying?"

("MBA.")

"Why Columbia?"

("My Princeton parents wanted a more citified experience.")
"What's your favorite part of business?"

("Innovation.")

"Which newspaper, if any, do your read?

("*Wall Street Journal* and *New York Times*.")

"How do you feel about my dear daughter, Serena?"

(After a three-second pause, he easily answered, "I love her.")

The rest of the dinner was kismet. Dad kidded his daughter for sitting on the sidelines of this two-way interview. "Have you anything to add?" he jibed to Serena.

"I don't know how I could get a word in edgewise." She laughed.

The rest of the meal was an easy repartee around wonderful cuisine. In the midst of it all, Chaz learned that his daughter and Tom had gone out for five months and had actually visited Chicago to visit with her mother.

"How is she?" Chaz asked.

"You two don't talk?"

"Not too frequently."

"She likes her studies. And she has a boyfriend."

"Really?"

"Some guy named Brad from the Art Institute." Serena shrugged.

After another sip of his Stoli, Chaz rolled his eyes and smiled at his daughter. "I should probably give her a call sometime and wish her well."

After espressos, he again expressed his pleasure to have had dinner with the young couple. He squired them to the street to make sure they could get a cab uptown to Columbia University.

Once they were safely on their way, Chaz Conner walked several lonely blocks downtown and pondered what kind of personal relationship, if any, might lie in his future.

CHAPTER 21

1982: A Marriage In The Family

The call from Tom Conley did not completely surprise Chaz Conner. Since their first meeting at Café des Artistes, Chaz had suspected that this union might actually transpire. After all, they seemed like a cute couple that enjoyed each other's company. They were both ambitious. They seemed to love Manhattan and each other.

"Might it be possible to meet you for a cup of coffee or a glass of wine?" the young man asked.

"Of course," Chaz answered.

The two men agreed to meet at the University Club on Fifty-Sixth Street at noon. Cognizant of club rules, both men wore suits and met at the bar. After a customary handshake, Tom Conley introduced his burning, top-of-mind topic.

"Mr. Conner, you know I think the world of your daughter."

"That's clearly evident."

"I would like your permission to ask her to be my wife." The young man instinctively took a deep breath and a sigh, as if he was relieved at the admission and the request.

More accustomed to negotiations, Chaz decided to let the young man twist, at least for a few seconds. He took a sip of his drink and then looked the young man in the eye. He then grinned. With a sense of the dramatic, he then uttered, "Wow, wow, wow." After another sip, he then gave the young man a hug. "I would be honored to have you as a member of this family."

In an involuntary release, Tom screamed "Hahhh. Yes!" as if there was ever a true question in the matter.

Through the remainder of the dinner, it was a genuine meeting of the minds. Chaz learned that his prospective son-in-law had always worked summers as a camp counselor in his hometown of Manhasset, New York. He discovered that his dad was an investment advisor and that his mom was a social worker. Tom planned to work on Wall Street after school, if possible. "I like the American capitalist system and would like to do something with it."

"It's a tough competitive gig, from what I hear," Chaz offered.

"Yeah, but from what I hear, so is the broadcastiing business," Tom countered.

"Touché," the future father-in-law acknowledged.

In exchange, the young man discovered that Chaz had been singlehandedly raised by his mother, and was devastated by her sudden death from a heart attack a decade ago. In a rare but telling reveal, Chaz felt comfortable talking to the young man about his mother's patience, guidance, and unconditional love. "She was always so worried about me in the war, but always in my corner. If it weren't for her, I would have never gone into journalism," he confessed. "What a wonderful woman," he then reflected, felt a glitch in his throat, and atypically fell silent.

After a few drinks and eggs Benedicts, the two men discussed the absolute appeal of Serena (so kind, so understanding, so smart), a few views on politics (of which the two men were not chasms apart), and the logistics of the upcoming wedding.

As was discussed, it would happen in April of 1983. Given the fact that neither Serena nor Tom were fervent Catholics, and the wedding is customarily in the fiancée's city, Leah had arranged the church (St. Clement's, where she and Chaz had been married). In an attempt to avoid a complete déjà vu experience, she suggested that the reception be at the School of the Art Institute of Chicago ballroom. Why?

1. It was convenient to the wedding ceremony.
2. It captured her mother's interest in psychological art therapy and would probably be a plus in her master's program.

3. It did capture her new interest in Brad Johansson, who was the membership director at the Art Institute.
4. 4. Most importantly, Leah did think it would be a great venue for a celebration in the city of Chicago.

At the reception, Chaz did give a wonderful tribute—to his daughter, to his ex-wife, but mostly to his new son-in-law. Having experienced decades of Nielsen ratings, he had learned that generous acknowledgments reflected beautifully on the beneficent benefactor. It was not as calculated as that last sentence might imply. Chaz did appreciate his new son-in-law, and while he had never had much opportunity to say so in the past few years, he did value all that his ex-wife, Leah, had done to keep their daughter centered and focused on the right things.

His accolades to Serena were the most touching.

"I remember when she was a little girl, and would smile at me when I walked through the door after a hard day at the office. I promise you I would melt every single night. Maybe there's nothing like that cocked-head giggle and glee from a daughter to a father. I have missed it for many years (especially since she turned nine or ten years old, and ceased being a little girl). But she still has that smile, just a little more grown-up now. And she has never lost her affection, her love, and her big heart. I fully assume that much of that will now be transferred to Tom, and I tell you, dear son-in-law, you are a lucky man to have it. However, dear Serena, I think you have a big enough heart to still send those vibes my way every once in a while, as I will always do to you. Best wishes to you both. I believe this will be one damn, amazing marriage. And I plan to be around a long time to witness it."

Later that night, Chaz asked his ex-wife, Leah, for a dance. She had been on the floor quite a bit with her new beau, Brad, whom she had met at the Art Institute of Chicago. He seemed like a nice enough guy, but it was always a little weird to see your former wife of decades with a different man, at least the first time. However, as Chaz reminded himself, *life moves on.* More to the point, life had moved on. After all, they had been divorced for two years and rarely spoke about anything other than financial matters. However, this was a night to celebrate family. So he asked for the honor of a dance in front of her new man-friend, Brad.

"That would be nice," Leah responded. She took her ex-husband's hand and led him to the center of the floor. As luck would have it (or not have it), the band decided to play "I'll Be Seeing You." Given the wording of the lyrics, it ended up being an emotional dance, particularly for Leah.

> *In the small café,*
> *The park across the way,*
> *The children's carousel,*
> *The chestnut tree,*
> *The wishing well.*
> *I'll be seeing you on every bright and sunny day ...*
> *I'll always think of you that way.*

It was the first time they had been so physically close in years. However, that did not explain the rush of emotion. It was all about the recollections of their young daughter growing up in a happy house. Halfway through the dance and the lyric, Chaz brought out a handkerchief and offered it to Leah. Rather gallantly, he also said, "We must complete this dance. C'mon, just follow my steps." They did. Regaining her composure by the end of the song, Leah did bow to her ex and throw a kiss to her daughter. The guests at all the tables did applaud.

If possible, the daddy-daughter dance was even more arresting. It was to the Sinatra hit called "The Way You Look Tonight." Once upon a time, when Chaz could practice piano, he would play it for his daughter.

As he hinted in his toast, his young daughter would look in his eyes and find inside tickles. In this particular case, she would sit on the same piano bench and try to create duets with her dad. He would bang out the notes. He would sing, and she would sing. And they would do their best to be on the same key.

At this wedding reception, there would be no off-key notes. The band impeccably played daddy and daughter's favorite song:

Someday, when I'm awfully low.
When the world is cold.
I will feel a glow just thinking of you
And the way you look tonight.

Somehow in the midst of this event, all the other guests allowed dad and daughter to have this precious time on the floor. No one dared intrude on the moment.

It was about as good a wedding ceremony as could ever be.

It was as happy as Chaz had been personally in ten years.

At the age of fifty-seven, it was also prime time to reconsider some vague thoughts about coasting toward retirement. A watershed moment like this reminded him that life can unfold at any age, especially if one wants it to happen.

CHAPTER 22

1985: Check Your Egos At The Door

For the next several years, Chaz Conner burnished his image as the premier host of broadcast magazines. With his excellent supporting cast, he was able to maintain good quality for his twice-weekly *What's Next?* ABC broadcast and still retain the ability to accomplish at least two or three interview segments of his own each week.

Here are his most noteworthy interviews:

* On the heels of the Harrods bombing in 1983, he was able to secure an exclusive interview with Sir Frederick Bruce, the British ambassador to the US, who admitted that "these hostilities between the IRA and Mother England will most likely not end soon." Within twenty-four hours, the Queen contradicted his statement and announced hope that sometime soon, we who speak the English language may all live in peace.

* He interviewed Malcolm Lowell Jr., the labor secretary under President Reagan, about the 12 percent unemployment rate, the highest figure since 1941. "Well, people just have to look a little harder to be gainfully employed," was the man's response.

* An interview with Mitt Romney, who was just appointed the head of the upcoming Los Angeles Olympic Games, also gained repeat airings since Mr. Romney admitted on the air that the Soviet bloc would be boycotting the games

in retaliation of the US boycott of their Moscow games four years earlier.

"However, I predict the most successful Olympics in the history of the games," Romney confidently stated. As it turned out, he was right.

However, the most tantalizing and circuitous scoop came as a result of a story about the famine in Africa. As Chaz had learned through years in the news business, stories this far from home do not normally attract an attentive audience. However, he had also learned that pop culture was the new normal, and this particular cause had the potential to veer into that angle.

The interview was with Harry Belafonte, the beloved African-American who always seemed sunny and was immortalized with his "Day-O." The interview started out as a celeb toast but quickly turned into an urgent call for relief. In his even-then whispery voice, Harry explained that the drought in Ethiopia had already claimed a million people, who had miserably died of starvation. "The UK has already come to the fore with a video called 'Do They Know It's Christmas.' But I believe that the US is the most generous country on this planet ... and I intend to mount a campaign for humanitarian aid to this part of the world."

"Well, please let us know how this proceeds," Chaz answered.

As he had learned over the last ten years, *What's Next?* had a powerful microphone. If he could magnify that, it would be good for the show and for his own persona.

Two weeks later, Harry Belafonte called the show and was able to connect with Chaz Conner.

"Remember that interview we had about famine in Africa?"

"Yes, of course I do," Chaz answered.

"Well, some wheels are turning. And I would suggest you get an interview with Quincy Jones, who just may—and this is off the record—record the biggest collection of music singers ever to try to address famine in the world. Here's his number."

Within three weeks, Quincy Jones was allotted an eight-minute slot on the fast-moving *What's Next?* show. After a few minutes of pleasantries, Chaz grilled him.

Chaz: I understand you are concerned about the famine in Africa.

Quincy: As should we all be, as citizens of this world.

Chaz: Do the rich people in Hollywood and in the music business really care about this?

Quincy: Well, perhaps we will see.

Chaz: Do you have plans to unite the creative community out West to make a movie about this—or a TV special, or a concert?

Quincy: We simply want to raise the consciousness of the problem in the best way possible.

It was that kind of cat-and-mouse game until Chaz revealed a ninety-second video on the severity of the problem in Africa. It showcased starving children with distended bellies and mothers crying out for help.

"Thank you for raising attention to this tragedy." Quincy Jones extended his hand to the host and added, "Perhaps with your help, we can change the world."

"Wouldn't that be nice? Wouldn't that be a wonderful *What's Next?* consequence for people who really need food to survive?"

As the set dimmed, Quincy Jones again reiterated his appreciation that Chaz had upped the ante on the issue. When the two men went into the wings, Quincy quizzed him, "I get the sense this isn't just about ratings."

"If it were just about ratings, I would never do a story on Ethiopia," Chaz quipped. "No, no, no … this is a human tragedy that must be addressed."

"You've got the right attitude," Quincy told him.

"Anything I can do to help, let me know," Chaz responded sincerely.

"I just may do that. If you get a call from Quincy, return it. You might have to get on a plane in a matter of hours, but it will probably be worth it."

"You've got a deal," the newsman responded.

In January 25 of 1985, there was one of those pink "While You Were Out" messages on Chaz Conner's desk. It indicated a call from Quincy Jones, with a return phone number.

Quincy Jones's message was succinct and mysterious:

If you can get out to LA on the evening of January 28, you will have a magical, humanitarian evening and the exclusive broadcast scoop of your life. However, you can't tell anyone about this until March. Not even your cohorts at ABC. All the entertainers are sworn to secrecy. You can bring one cameraman and one microphone, but nothing else. When you get to LA, call me from your hotel, and I will tell you where to go. I figure if any broadcaster is big enough to be able to pull this off without squealing or leaking the information, it's you. I don't quite know why I trust you, but I do—and so does Harry Belafonte. So get your ass out here, and let's cover the biggest event of the decade.

In an unprecedented act, Chaz went to the legal department and asked for Mia Hanratty. He considered her the most trustworthy attorney in the place, especially since she had defended Chaz against several nuisance libel suits for comments he had made on air—all of which she had won without a financial settlement. Chaz liked dealing with her, partly because she was sharp-witted and easy on the eyes. Sort of like Annette Benning.

"I have a special request," Chaz declared. "I would like to cover a very secret story with a cameraman and sound recorder, but the subject is panicked about prematurely releasing the information. Can you draw up a contract for me, the cameraman, and the sound engineer that will reassure them that their secret is safe with us? I'm not a lawyer, but it should exert some sense of penalty if any leak is attributable to us."

"Sounds diabolically tantalizing," Mia responded. "What's the nature of the project?"

Chaz just laughed. "See, that's the thing. I can't tell anyone. Is that a trick question just to see if I can't keep a secret?"

"No, I'm just curious."

"It kills the cat," Chaz responded and began to enjoy the repartee.

"From a legal standpoint, I need to ask some pertinent questions: Does it involve any government secret? Does it include an exposé of a business that might consequently sue this network? Does it involve any international security questions, or even vague areas? Is there a risk toward ABC for libel or slander? Are you willing to vouch for the veracity of the contact and reimburse ABC for all expenses if this secret mission tends to be a wash?"

"The answers to all your questions are no, even the last one. I figure ABC should trust me on this one. If I blow it, they can fire me."

"I don't think they ever will," Mia responded.

"Well, you never know," Chaz admitted.

Mia then smiled at the newsman and gave him the cold, hard truth. "I will draw up three contracts that you can present to your 'subject.' Between the two of us, they may not be legally binding, but most people are persuaded by a legal contract, and it may scare anyone from leaking information."

"That will be enough," Chaz reacted.

"I wish I could be there for this secret 007 mission," Mia admitted.

"So come with me," Chaz responded. "I am not trying to immediately get in the sack with you—separate rooms. Although you are amazingly attractive. But I do find you intellectually interesting and amazingly attractive (just to repeat myself) … and it would be a big plus if I had a major attorney from ABC at my side as I tried to gain interviews from Michael Jackson, Lionel Richie, Billy Joel, and Bruce Springsteen."

"Tantalizing. You may need me to protect you from spilling the beans," Mia acknowledged.

It was the first time Chaz had been so forward since his college years. But sometimes, one "feels it." And Chaz was one who still, in his bones, liked to trust his instinct.

And so their first "date" was in LA, at the Westwood Marquis.

After acknowledging his whereabouts to Quincy Jones, Chaz and his small entourage agreed to come to the A&M Studios in Hollywood at 9:00 p.m. As further reassurance of security, Chaz announced that he had privately enlisted an attorney at ABC to assure confidentiality for the two crew people who would accompany him.

"You will need to stay out of glare," Quincy warned him. "Only you and *Life* magazine are allowed on the set. And the release date for any publicity is March 8."

"Agreed," Chaz answered. "And I will ultimately help the cause, as will *Life* magazine."

"That's why you are invited," Quincy pragmatically responded.

When Chaz, Mia, and his two techies reached the eerily desolate studio, they were confronted by a sign on the outside window of the building. It read, "Check your ego at the door."

When they tiptoed into the recording room, they looked through the glass and heard Michael Jackson recording his solo for "We Are the World." At this time, no filming was allowed. However, in the aftermath, Chaz did get a quote before the onslaught of talent descended upon the studio.

"What was your inspiration for this song?" Chaz asked.

In his whispery voice, Michael said that he and Lionel, in an attempt to create a worldwide anthem, had listened to dozens of national anthems— USA, UK, Canada, Germany, Australia, Mexico, France, etc. "It should be something everyone can feel, and everyone can sing," the pop icon said and then shyly walked away from the camera.

In the next half hour, an onslaught of talent appeared. There was Lionel Ritchie, Dionne Warwick, Billy Joel, Ray Charles, Diana Ross, Bruce Springsteen, Smokey Robinson, and scores of other luminaries. Let's make this easy, here were the soloists in their order of appearance:

Lionel Richie
Stevie Wonder
Paul Simon
Kenny Rogers
James Ingram
Tina Turner
Billy Joel
Michael Jackson
Diana Ross
Dionne Warwick
Willie Nelson
Al Jarreau
Bruce Springsteen

Kenny Loggins
Steve Perry
Daryl Hall
Huey Lewis
Cyndi Lauper
Kim Carnes
Bob Dylan
Ray Charles

In addition, there was an all-star chorus:

Dan Aykroyd
Harry Belafonte
Lindsey Buckingham
Mario Cipollina
Johnny Colla
Sheila E.
Bob Geldof
Bill Gibson
Chris Hayes
Sean Hopper
Jackie Jackson
La Toya Jackson
Marlon Jackson
Randy Jackson
Tito Jackson
Waylon Jennings
Bette Midler
John Oates
Jeffrey Osborne
Anita Pointer
June Pointer
Ruth Pointer
Smokey Robinson

That's forty-five superstars with amazing egos that surreptitiously
entered the studio and stood on their mark to record their single

lines (or duet lines). Bear in mind, no one on the stage knew the drift of the song, other than Quincy Jones, Lionel Richie, and Michael Jackson, who had only finished the song twenty-four hours before the recording date.

One by one (or two by two), the soloists would do their thing, and they were usually paired for the sake of contrast. For example, Willie Nelson with Dionne Warwick. Paul Simon with Kenny Rogers. Bruce Springsteen with Al Jarreau.

As Chaz Conner had discussed with Quincy Jones, he would only interview people off the stage. "I'm gonna have my hands full in the studio with forty- five egos, so I will need you to honor that. Same deal with *Life* magazine. No interviews on the soundstage. However, if your guy is good with a camera, it probably wouldn't hurt to capture the solos and duets when each of the singers have their moment in the sun."

The ABC cameraman Billy Benson did just that. Yes, Chaz told him to stay out of the way of the production ... as much as possible. In his twenty-two- year career at ABC, Benson had covered presidents, prime ministers, and kings and queens—so he knew how to get footage without sticking his camera in someone's face.

One by one, when the performers went to the greenroom, Chaz would have a moment or two with them. However, he did gain some amazing quotes:

Springsteen: "I believe in the cause, and I just wanted to be together with this group of like-minded people."

Willie Nelson: "It's a beautiful thing, isn't it ... when people come together for something bigger than showbiz fame?"

Diana Ross: "What an amazing song! What an amazing moment!"

Bob Dylan: "I tell you, I was a little nervous about this. It's such a big, swelling anthem—and that's not usually my style. But Quincy cooled me down. In his words, 'We just want you to be you.'"

Stevie Wonder: "I feel so proud to be here tonight."

Lionel Richie: "No, it was not difficult to write the song (laughs out loud). Coming up with one song that appeals to forty-five professionals in the music business is no challenge, especially when you are teamed with Michael Jackson (eye roll)."

After all the solos were recorded, and in the early morning hours, Stevie Wonder brought in two Ethiopian women who took the microphones and thanked the entertainers. They also explained that over one million of their fellow citizens had died of famine in the past two years. It gained a standing ovation.

As Quincy Jones had promised them in his "keep it quiet" invitation, when your kids or grandkids ask what you did for this world hunger crises, you can play this song.

At about four in the morning, Mia reached her hand toward Chaz and admitted, "This is one amazing evening. Are all of your first dates this good?"

"There has never been a more important, more impactful, more electric first date in the history of life," Chaz answered.

Instinctively, she reached across the chair and kissed him.

No one wanted to leave the soundstage. Ray Charles was recorded at that time for riffs and answers to the chorus. So was Stevie Wonder. At about that time, Kenny Rogers asked every performer to sign his sheet music. Diana Ross soon followed. This created an autograph medley, where every single performer wanted every other performer to sign their T-shirt or their sheet music. Somehow, all participants knew they were into something special.

On March 8, *What's Next?* telecasted a rare one-hour special from Chaz alone that corresponded with the *Life* magazine story of "We Are the World." As he had promised to Quincy Jones, he would not leak the info before the *Life* cover story. However, it was a blockbuster airing that was excerpted on many TV channels.

The electricity of the evening was captured in the show. It depicted artists sharing a purpose and celebrating the glee of that evening. The snippets of the soloists were arresting, as was the final montage of the song. Unlike most of his broadcasts, Chaz did little editorializing.

He ended his program with this thought:

"As the lyric suggests, 'There comes a time when we heed a certain call ... when the world must come together as one.' Perhaps this is that time. If you feel the urge—and I hope you do—then contribute. I have. And I hope you will do the same. People should not die for lack of food. Good night. Eat well. Give a damn."

Chaz often asked in his show, "What's next?" In this case, amazing things happened. Initial shipments of 800,000 records sold out in three days. It became the fastest-selling American pop single in history. It raised over 63 million dollars in famine relief (90 percent went to Africa, 10 percent was diverted to USA hunger and homelessness problems). The song was simultaneously broadcasted over eight thousand worldwide radio stations on April 8.

Even in a thirty-year-plus backward lens, the recording was a once-in-a- decade miracle. More honestly, it was perhaps a once-in-several-decades miracle. Never before or never since have so many singers and pop icons been brought together on one single night.

They were white.

They were black.

They were rock.

They were folk.

They were country.

They were Motown.

They were pop.

They were all together on one stage, in union, singing about the need to unite.

As the anthem begins, "There comes a time when we heed a certain call, when the world must come together as one."

On one night—January 28, 1985—the music community of America joined as one, checked their egos at the door, and sang their hearts out to eradicate world hunger.

CHAPTER 23

1989: Pandora's Box

Ever since he had survived the Normandy invasion, endured the Korean conflict, and studied Khrushchev's "We will bury you" speeches, Chaz Conner had convinced himself that the Cold War would be the permanent status quo.

Ironically, Ronald Reagan began to thaw this freeze. One step was an initiative called the "Star Wars" defense. It always struck Chaz as a gimmick, since it was named after the Hollywood movie starring Harrison Ford, Chewbacca, and a robot called R2D2. Supposedly, it could destroy Russian missiles in midair, before they ever descended on the Empire State Building.

The less farcical bombshell was the speech that the president delivered on June 12, 1987, the 750th anniversary of Berlin. On the border of East and West Berlin, in a very clear and assertive voice worthy of an Oscar, Reagan addressed the Russian leader (who was not there at the time). His famous words: "Mr. Gorbachev, tear down this wall!"

It became the most repeated, reprinted, and broadcasted passage since FDR's promise that "The only thing we have to fear is fear itself." The fact that it was often compared to FDR's brave stance against the Nazis only added credence to the quote.

According to legend, there was actually some debate about whether or not the sentence "went too far." Some of Reagan's advisors thought the speech was strong enough without this barb. Others recommended that the president include it. Evidently,

Reagan finally called the shot and defended it in simple terms. "Hey, Gorbachev really should tear down that damned wall."

Despite Conner's left-leaning tendencies, he did admire the president's cojones on this subject. Consequently, he booked sympathetic guests on his program. Ed Meese III, the counselor to the president, was proud of Reagan for "taking the hard line and pushing back at the Russian bullies." Arguably, this ran the risk of inflaming the issue even further. Colin Powell, his national security advisor, was more evenhanded. "We will watch Russia closely. Hopefully, we can reach an accommodation for the good of all people." As was his custom, it tended to say nothing; but it sounded good.

The big interview of the week was with Vice-President George H. W. Bush, who had led the CIA, served as Reagan's VP, and was clearly aligned to be the next president. "Gotta be prudent," Bush said. "Gotta be vigilant. Gotta defend American interests." By god, it almost sounded like a preview of the comedic imitations that *SNL*'s Dana Carvey would employ in portraying the man.

In a stroke of incredibly prophetic timing, Chaz had convinced the producers of *What's Next?* that it might be advantageous to anchor the show from the Berlin Wall in early November of 1989. As had been leaked to him from sources inside East Germany, there was a good chance that the wall would soon fall.

He asked Mia to accompany him on this event. True, she would have to put in for a week's vacation ... but as Chaz predicted, this might just be worth it. "Besides, it would be fun to have some time with you, away from the office." After a day of clearing her schedule in the legal department of ABC, the two of them boarded a red-eye special to West Berlin and checked into the Leonardo Hotel, which was just a few steps from the Brandenburg Gate.

The world was clearly and quickly changing. In 1997, Estonia demanded autonomy from the Soviet Union. Lithuania and Latvia quickly followed. Soon afterward, civil unrest against Moscow had erupted in Poland and Hungary. Mikhail Gorbachev had even tried to push a concept called "glasnost," which allowed for some civil disobedience but also was a risky move for the long-term health of the Soviet Union. But there were signs everywhere that his hold on this fragile empire was crumbling. In 1989, Gorbachev and newly elected president George H. W. Bush jointly declared the end of the Cold War.

However, the wall still stood between East and West Germany.

On November 7, 1989, Chaz and Mia had dinner at Café Wintergarten in Literaturhaus, Berlin. As is often underestimated in global culinary circles, the German food was spectacular. They shared schnitzel and spaetzle, washed it down with a few bottles of Beck's beer, and felt completely comfortable in the candlelit booth, despite jet jag and the daunting prospect that the next forty-eight hours might be nonstop news days.

One of the things that attracted Chaz to her was the fact that Mia, in addition to being a smart corporate lawyer, enjoyed the news. "This city is great," she opined. "Can't imagine the flip side across the wall in East Germany."

"It's not pretty," Chaz responded.

"Been there?"

"A long, long time ago … before it was even called *East* Berlin," Chaz said, recalling his European missions during WWII. "I hear it is grim these days. But hey, it's supposed to all change while we are here."

"You know, this whole thing is Pandora's box," she offered. Once it's opened, everything unfolds, explodes, and tumbles out. There's no going back. You can't put the toothpaste back in the tube."

"I love the way you completely mix metaphors," Chaz answered and toasted her. Afterward, they did get a good night's sleep before the hammer- wielding local citizens began to destroy the last remaining symbol of the Cold War.

The wall began as a fence. By 1989, it had become a four-foot-wide, three- hundred-foot barrier patrolled by soldiers with German shepherd dogs, surveilled by watchtowers, and protected with minefields. Many people had attempted to scale it (it's estimated that five thousand did succeed). However, many more were slain in their attempts to escape to the West.

On November 9, 1989, in a further nod to *glasnost,* the East German government announced that all their citizens could visit

West Germany and West Berlin. It marked the first time in twenty-eight years that separated family members on either side of the wall could actually touch each other. Not surprisingly, it resulted in an event viewed all over the world.

Within hours, people came to the wall with sledgehammers and chisels. Unless you are totally asleep at the historical wheel, you have seen this spontaneous celebration. Local citizens chipped off souvenirs. They crushed lengthy concrete sections. They reunited with long-lost family, cousins they had not seen for decades.

If this were a movie, it would win an Academy Award. Fortunately, it was better than a movie. It was real life, and it was happening before the eyes of the world.

With his film crew, Chaz was on the site to capture the event. He found family members tearfully communicating with each after so many decades apart ... through cracks and holes in the wall. He witnessed and commented on fathers and their children hammering away at the twenty-eight-year chasm. His reportorial coup was the film of an East German soldier helping an eighty-year-old woman across the ruins of the recently collapsed barricade. This particular segment ended with the soldier waving to the old woman's welcoming family on the West side.

Chaz Conner ended his report with an emotional wallop. "As a dear friend of mine told me the other night, this is Pandora's box. It has now been opened. What flows from this is actually up to us—on the East and on the West. It could be the dawning of a great new day. Or it could simply be a happy pause, as we a slide back to old tensions and uncomfortable geopolitical chess games. In the midst of this celebration, we must hope for the former. It is happy! It is contagious! It is wonderful!"

When Roone Arledge saw the feed, he held both hands in the air and privately congratulated himself that he had the foresight to hire the most compelling, most spontaneous wordsmith on TV news. That was ten years ago, but Roone had never been prouder of an ABC broadcast—or America.

That evening, at the Gottlob Restaurant in the Schoenberg district of West Germany, Chaz and Mia shared a dinner of pork tenderloin and asparagus, accompanied by some fine German white wine.

At a certain point, the waitress brought over a bottle of champagne.

"Yes, I congratulate you on a wonderful report," a surprised Mia said at this surprise offering.

"No, this is not for me," Chaz answered. "It's for us." He then watched patiently as the waitress poured the contents into two champagne flutes. Before Mia could bring the glass to her lips, he reached in his pocket and put a small package in the middle of the table.

On the cover of the box, there was a handwritten message. It read, *From Pandora.*

"Open it," he urged.

She did so and discovered a sparkling ring from a local West German jewelry store.

"I am not a young man," the sixty-six-year-old journalist admitted. "And I never imagined I would ever marry again. But this weekend, together with you, and together with the falling wall, I am filled with optimism. I am in love with you. As I said on last night's broadcast, 'It's happy. It's contagious. It's wonderful.' Here's what I didn't say in front of the viewing audience: I would never want it to end. So let's make this happen. We may as well laugh together officially." He then paused, and as a true Midwestern-raised gentleman, he looked her straight in the eye and asked, "Will you marry me?"

Mia, with a great sense of the dramatic, took a slow sip of her champagne and looked back at Chaz. She then moved her chair back and walked over to the man. Slowly and passionately, she kissed him on the lips and said, "Yes. I thought you'd never ask."

CHAPTER 24

1995: It Was A Very Good Year

It is always dangerous to dub a twelve-month period a universally sweet, sweet time. After all, some dear dads died, some women were denied advancements, some teenagers were bullied, and some minorities were inevitably incarcerated (often unjustly).

However, for Chaz Conner—the host of the popular ABC newsmagazine called *What's Next?*—it was a banner year. The show continued to be in the top three of all news programs (and the top twenty of all network programming) despite its grueling twice-a-week schedule. Add to this the fact that Chaz, at the ripe age of seventy-one, had found and enjoyed love with his new wife, Mia. After six years of marriage, it felt as strong as any emotion he had ever enjoyed. Often, they would have romantic evenings in Manhattan. Sometimes they would visit Broadway. Often, they would share professional challenges and laughs late at night in a local pub or in their Murray Hill kitchen.

While Chaz had happily spread the workload of his show among his young correspondents, he still commanded many of the scoops of the year. Just one day prior to the Oscars, for example, he had a coup interview with Tom Hanks, who was the odds-on favorite to win the best actor award for his role in *Forrest Gump.*

"Do you not think it's a real stretch that Forrest has participated in so many world-event stories?" Chaz asked the actor.

"No, not at all. Newsmen do that all the time. You were there for a Kennedy interview. The assassination in Dallas. "We Are the World." The Berlin Wall. Does that make you Forrest Gump?"

"No, but I was there to ask questions, find facts, and report on the moment," Chaz rebutted. "Not just as an idiot savant who happened to be photobombing the scene."

"I would not call Forrest Gump an idiot savant," Tom Hanks protested.

"What would you call him?"

"I would call him an innocent. The man does not have a mean bone in his body and just happened to be at the right place at the right time—many times."

"Was such a character difficult for you to play?" Chaz wondered.

"Not for me. Did you ever see the movie *Big*? If so, you might know, I am pretty innocent at heart."

Chaz chuckled. "Do you think you will win the Oscar tomorrow night?

What would your Forrest Gump character predict?"

"That's easy," Tom Hanks responded with a smile. "Life is just a box of chocolates. You never know what you are going to get."

The newsman's next coup was in Oklahoma City on April 19. He had heard across the newswires that there had been a major case of domestic terrorism. Rather than wait for all the details, that new lead was tantalizing enough for him to gather a recording crew and film crew to reach the Midwestern city ASAP. By 2:00 p.m., they were the first national news crew on the scene, and the first to report that Timothy McVeigh had been stopped by an Oklahoma state trooper for driving without a license plate and for illegal weapons possessions. Shortly thereafter, he and Terry Nichols were linked by forensic evidence as the perpetrators of this crime.

In the carnage behind his report, there were 160 dead bodies and 650 injured people. The blast shattered glass in 258 nearby buildings and shocked the entire community.

At 9:00 p.m., Chaz Conner soberly reported:

"For the first time, evidently, a homegrown terrorist has taken revenge on his own fellow citizens and decided to blow them to smithereens. Behind me is the result of this odious act—the Alfred

P. Murrah Federal Building ripped apart by a series of explosives. More devastating, there are bodies strewn across the landscape … and dare I say parts of bodies, including those of women and young children who just happened to be in the building at the time of this evil act.

"At the time, we do not have a motive. But two men—Timothy McVeigh and Terry Nichols—have been apprehended. It will take months to learn what made their sick minds tick. It will take forever for the survivors and the spouses and parents of victims to ever understand what in the world happened here in Oklahoma City on April 19. What did it prove? What was the idea behind this awful act? Most importantly, as we often ask on this program, 'What's next?' I shudder to even contemplate an answer to that question. Let me at least start with this hope, some serious reflection about who we are as a people and what value we place on those strangers around us … who, in the final analysis, are not all that different than we are. This is Chaz Conner promising to stay here for several days and at least start to answer those questions. Good night. Hug someone you love. God bless them, and God bless America."

His next big story of the year was more predictable.

The O. J. Simpson trial had captivated the nation, and no matter how it turned out, it was as ghoulishly fascinating as watching the former footballer's getaway drive on the LA Freeway in his Ford Bronco with a gun supposedly pointed to his head. "Will he kill himself? Will he kill those around him? Will he try to escape to Mexico? Will he return to his Westwood home?"

Once the trial began, everyone knew it would be a circus. There was Marcia Clark, Christopher Darden, and Mark Furman, the detective on the case who was accused of using the "N" word.

On OJ's side of the aisle, there was a dream team of lawyers—F. Lee Bailey, Robert Shapiro, Alan Dershowitz, Robert Kardashian, Johnny Cochrane, and Barry Scheck, among others.

And on the bloody sidewalk of home were the victims—Nicole Brown Simpson and a young man named Ron Goldman.

The trial went on for four months and was the best soap opera on daytime TV. Judge Ito seemed to like the drama and the spotlight and helped contribute to the pop culture phenomenon of this ugly murder mystery.

When the defense began to wind down, Chaz Conner reluctantly agreed to cover the verdict for ABC news. "What's the point?" he first protested. "There is no scoop here. Every news team from Syracuse to Santa Fe is covering this trial."

"And if we are not there, we are missing America's favorite story of the year," Roone Arledge reminded him. "It's the price of fame. You'll find an angle."

Chaz decided to visit the LA courthouse and join the vast media entourage, as long as he could go with Mia and enjoy some of Tinseltown. The couple stayed at Shutters on the Beach in Santa Monica, and did enjoy some evening with Rita Wilson and Tom Hanks, whom Chaz celebrated with a toast for his Oscar-worthy performance as Forrest Gump. As a greeting gift, Chaz even brought the star and his wife two boxes of chocolates.

On other free nights, Chaz and Mia enjoyed some Hollywood premiers —*Toy Story, Apollo 13,* and *The Bridges of Madison County*—along with some dinners at Chasen's, Mario's, and Michael's.

However, it wasn't all showbiz. Given the onslaught of coverage, Chaz had been thinking of some angle and decided that his best bet was Fred Goldman, the grieving and angry father of the young man who lost his life just because he worked at Mezzaluna, the restaurant Nicole had visited that night with her mother and where she had left a pair of glasses on the table. Evidently, the waiter offered to deliver the glasses to Nicole's condo. According to all accounts, Ron was an innocent young man who just happened to be in the wrong place at the wrong time.

From his background breakfast interviews with Mr. Goldman, Chaz knew that his sound bites could be explosive. All the lawyers would be guarded, as would the prosecution team. However, Mr. Goldman believed that O. J. Simpson was "the killer" and would only order orange juice for breakfast, rather than ever again say the word "OJ."

On the air for one interview, Fred Goldman explained his version of the case, "My son walked into a murder in progress, and he lost his life. Ron was the hero. He was my hero. Someone like that should be remembered and honored. Justice must prevail here. People should not be able to get away with murder."

Never one to mince words, Fred Goldman normally looked like he was about to pop a blood vessel whenever he talked about O. J. Simpson. On days when the tide tended to favor the former footballer—such as the famous gloves fitting (or not fitting)—Goldman's interview with Chaz Conner was laced with fury and frustration.

"Give me a break! The guy has been an actor for the past ten years. That grimace on his face when he tried to put on his bloody gloves? A performance. An overacted one, but just as ridiculous as the man himself. I just hope the jury is smart enough not to buy into that bogus act of his. This man is bad. He's a double-murderer, and his legal team is doing our justice system a disservice by trying shenanigans such as this. It's crazy. It's crap. It's bullshit."

Of course, the last two words were bleeped on the broadcast, but it was quite an interview, punctuated by the fact that Fred Goldman walked away from the spot after his last two expletives, and the camera captured him waving his hands to the heavens as he tried to reconcile the surreal aspect of this trial with his desire for a conviction.

When the "not guilty" verdict was delivered on October 3, 1995, OJ and his dream team of lawyers were filmed smiling and hugging each other. By contrast, Fred Goldman was captured in shock and pain. It was replayed on every news station across the nation. It was, of course, widely assumed that Chaz Conner would get the scoop. Instead, grief won. After a few moments, Mr. Goldman and his daughter Kim, in tears, swept by the throng of reporters and also by Chaz.

"Mr. Goldman, can we get a reaction?"

"You saw it in the courtroom," the anguished father acknowledged. "No more questions. No more. No more."

In a rare moment of journalistic reticence, Chaz Conner decided to honor the father's need for privacy. Instead, that night, he reported on the "disturbingly different" reactions to this verdict:

"Among the black citizens, it is widely seen as a prejudicial case of police malfeasance and planted evidence. Among white citizens, it is predominately viewed as a miscarriage of justice, despite an avalanche of evidence … on the part of celebrity and legal tricks. However, the verdict is in: not guilty. What's next? Hopefully, a little more harmony between the races and some understanding that not everything needs to be viewed through the prism of black vs. white. However, I am not holding my breath. I simply hold out hope."

That night, Chaz Conner and his wife, Mia, dined at Mezzaluna, as a symbolic memorial to Ron Goldman and Nicole Brown Simpson. It was a quiet dinner while both liberal-leaning individuals whispered about the implications of the case.

"I looked around today and suddenly thought most black people, who were silently smiling in groups on the sidewalk, must secretly resent me … as if I am the one who ever used the 'N' word in my life, which I have never done," Mia admitted.

"I know," Chaz answered and extended his hand to his wife. "I actually think this may set back race relations in the country for at least a decade. And that makes me weary."

After a pause, Mia looked around the dining room, and then reached out and touched her husband's hand. "I think you did a great job and a great service in reporting the story. And I know you weren't even that keen to cover this particular circus."

"Well, maybe there is something to be said for experience and age." Chaz then took a sip of water and returned the touch to his loved one. "Otherwise, I would have never met you."

"At least, we've got each other," she offered.

"And that is major." Chaz smiled.

In the background, the old hit from Frank Sinatra played:

> *I think of my life as vintage wine*
> *From fine old kegs,*
> *From the brim to the dregs*
> *It poured sweet and clear.*
> *It was a very good year.*

CHAPTER 25

2001: There's A Fire In The Sky

By mid-June of 2001, at the ripe age of seventy-six, veteran newsman Chaz Conner had begun to think of slowing down. Admittedly, many broadcast journalists extended their broadcasting lives into their seventies and eighties.

Eric Severeid, for one, continued to report in his late eighties and early nineties. Mike Wallace continued to report for *60 minutes*, and he did so well into his late eighties. Later on, Barbara Walters reported into her mideighties.

However, Chaz Conner had other considerations. Unlike the aforementioned newspeople, Chaz was an on-the-road correspondent. For the past thirty years, he had travelled about 120 days a year for assignment jobs and had begun to feel the fatigue of jet lag. He had a wonderful marriage with Mia and longed to spend more time with her. Also, his daughter and grandson were in Manhattan, and he often wished he had more casual get-togethers than the appointments they would make weeks in advance.

He still had a true drive and devotion for the news, but did not want to endure any whispers of a downhill decline. Consequently, he scheduled a lunch with his ABC boss, Roone Arledge, to discuss the future. As usual, it was at Michael's on Fifty-Fourth Street.

"Don't tell me you want even more money," Roone kidded him.

"No, maybe even less money," Chaz surprisingly answered. He then explained that he honestly thought it might be time to pass the torch to a new group of hungry newsmen.

"You're still hungry," Roone protested, "and the show still gets great ratings, thanks to you. I don't want to give that up."

"Well, I don't either, really … but I think it's time. I can hang in until the end of the year, at which time you figure out a great send-off for me. And, Roone, you are the best guy in the world at reinventing a news genre. You'll figure out a way. You always have."

Roone took a drink of his vodka and let all this sink in. Quite honestly, he had not expected this turn of events; but he had learned that in the media business, surprises were a way of life. After a swig, he made a counteroffer.

"Chaz, here is a better deal. I will honor your desires partway. We continue on as is until the end of the year, at which time we revamp the show, and you become anchor emeritus for both *What's Next?* and the *ABC Evening News*. I'm thinking six in-depth feature stories a year. At least half of them can be on your schedule."

"Mmmm." Chaz Conner smiled, and his eyes twinkled at the possibility of a more relaxed schedule that could keep him connected to the journalism field, which he always loved.

"What else are you going to do? Walk the beach with a metal detector? Play pickup games of chess down at Union Square? Shop? C'mon, Chaz … you have too much affection for this field and too much expertise to simply walk away. We can work on a more relaxed schedule, which might be good for you and for the network."

"I like the idea," Chaz admitted.

"But until January 1, we keep this quiet. And you continue as the anchor extraordinaire for every broadcast of *What's Next?*. Agreed?"

Chaz extended his glass of wine to Roone's glass, and they clinked. He then said, "Agreed. Hell, for all we know, we might have a great story or two between now and the end of the year."

On September 11, that event presented itself.

Chaz Conner was walking from his Murray Hill apartment at 8:00 a.m. on an unusually sunny autumn morning. It normally took him about twenty minutes to get to Lincoln Square, but about halfway through his journey, he heard the sound of a low-flying jet. He looked up the skyline of Midtown Manhattan and saw a jumbo jet flying way too close to the skyscrapers. His human instinct told him "Wow, that's unusual." His journalism chops screamed "Something is wrong!" He immediately picked up his pace and reached the ABC newsroom in a huff and a hurry.

"Emergency. Emergency. I need a van, a news camera, and a sound guy ASAP. We need to head downtown. Something is wrong, and I want ABC to be the first with the story!"

It was a rare command from Chaz Conner, who normally did not bark out orders. Given the contradiction, the newsroom did snap to attention and get on the road within six or seven minutes. Along the West Side Highway, they simply followed the billow of smoke that seemed to be rising from Lower Manhattan. By eight forty, they had arrived at the scene, and the cameraman —a pro named Billy Benson (who had been on the "We Are the World"

shoot)—started loading film in anticipation of who knows what.

By the time the trio exited the ABC van, another plane was flying low and seemed to be headed to Tower 2. From wartime experience, Billy Benson knew that he should aim his camera at the projectile. Within a few seconds, he was able to focus on the airliner and witness it crashing into the second tower. He was the first and only cameraman to film this tragedy (other than some primitive home cameras).

Within the next ten minutes, Chaz was wired with a microphone and standing in front of a chaotic disaster scene. Surrounding him was mayhem. Police cars were screeching to a halt. Fire trucks were pulling into the square, and the officers were racing toward the bedlam in full riot gear. At the same time, clouds of gray smoke were wafting in every direction.

5-4-3-2 … On cue, Chaz Conner began the first network broadcast:

"We are down here at the base of the World Trade Center, where something is wrong. Let me correct that—something is very, very wrong. At 8:14 this morning, an airplane crashed into America's most famous business structure. At first, we thought it might be an accident. At least, we could hope so. But within the next half hour, another plane crashed into Tower 2. According to most experts, it's nearly impossible to believe that this is nothing less than an orchestrated strike on America.

"As you can hear from the emergency vehicles behind me, this is a major dramatic catastrophe. At this point, we don't know why it happened, or exactly how … but as your first network on the scene, we will do our best to find out. Stay tuned. Say a prayer. This is morning rush hour in New York, and people inside those burning buildings need all the help they can get."

One hour later, he was back on the air with a news bulletin:

"Just a few minutes ago, the entire west tower of the World Trade Center just collapsed, creating a gray-out of smoke … and untold deaths. This city— and, in fact, the entire nation—is in disbelief that such an attack could cripple an entire nation. At 9:08, all airplanes were banned from taking off at any NYC airports. At 9:21, all bridges and tunnels were closed. At 9:37, another jet crashed into the Pentagon in Washington DC. It's as if the entire nation is under siege."

As he spoke, the scene became very smoky; and when it cleared, viewers could see that the veteran newsman was covered with soot and ash from the building collapse. "We do have exclusive footage of the United 175 as it struck Tower 2. Look at this amazing act of terrorism. Wait! Wait! I just have it that a fourth plane has just been crashed. Oh my goodness. This one fell from the skies in Somerset, Pennsylvania, just southeast of Pittsburgh. We pray that there will be no other catastrophes, but as anyone who has been listening to me knows by now, the disasters are coming in cascades. Just to repeat the big news here from ground zero, Tower 1 has just collapsed, and …"

At that time, we could see Chaz Conner listen to his feed. "Yes, yes, yes. Evidently, the police are asking us to move from this spot, as it is a potential danger zone. We will give you as much information as we can until we are forced to—"

And then, suddenly, the sound was lost. The cameraman did pan to his left and capture the other tower in a thundering state of collapse. Then there was mayhem in the camera and a whoosh of engulfing gray smoke. And then gray and white ashes occupied the camera lens.

After about five excruciating seconds, the broadcast resumed from the studio—in the ABC Studios uptown. Jon Scott, one of the young correspondents of *What's Next?*, addressed the camera soberly, "We don't quite know what happened there at the location, but we have lost connection with our crew and our beloved anchorman, Chaz Conner. According to some adept camerawork from our camera hero, Billy Benson, it appears as if the second World Trade Center tower has fallen. At this time, we have no confirmation of this, but Benson appeared to have captured the collapse on film … until our entire crew was disconnected. Oh boy."

In a rare moment of on-air emotion, Scott gulped and continued, "This is a brave crew, and we hope and pray that everyone is safe. Meanwhile, we will fill you in on other developments on this horrific day."

For the next forty-five minutes, the ABC studios reported the roller coaster of events. There was footage of President George W. Bush being interrupted with the news while reading a children's story to a kindergarten class. There were reports that he was now en route to Washington DC … but there were also reports that Cheney and the Defense staff had been taken to a secure location. There were also rumors that a Mideastern terrorist group had been linked to the multiple attacks. And of course, there were plenty of shocked faces from the remote broadcasts in Grand Central Station, Penn Station, and the Pentagon.

"Hold on. Hold on. We have some good news," Jon Scott interrupted the broadcast. "We have Chaz Conner on the line right now—the bravest man in broadcasting—along with his inveterate crew who have survived the collapse of Tower 2. Chaz? Are you there?"

When the camera revealed the man, he looked as if he had miraculously outlived Pompeii. He was completely covered—head to toe—in white and gray dust. His dark suit and white shirt were now a monochromatic light gray. Even his eyebrows were dusted.

"Jon, we are fine," Chaz reported, suddenly and automatically switching into his journalistic mode. "But I fear to say that many of the people trapped in that building are no longer fine. It was an awful collapse, and you have to believe that there were many trapped people in that building. Whoever diabolically engineered this event must be a very sick person. Let us get our bearings here, and we will have more reports. We will try to ascertain casualties, the whys and the wherefores, and try our best, as always, to answer the question: *What's Next?"*

At 2:30 p.m., he alerted the network that he might have a chance to gain a sound bite from Rudolph Giuliani, who had acted instantly and—by most bipartisan accounts—smartly about the catastrophe. Chaz questioned, "Mr. Mayor, do you have any estimate of the amount of people who lost their lives today?"

On his way to meet with the police and fire department, he did slow his step just enough to answer and perhaps brace the people in this city. "I don't want to speculate about that, but it's more than any of us can bear."

By 10:00 p.m. that evening, Chaz had his last report of September 11, 2001. With some flair for the theatrical, he had refused to clean up his suit or even wipe the ash from his hair or eyebrows. Like a ghost from a gray snowstorm, he reported, "We have had a miserable event happen today, akin to Pearl Harbor. Who knows how many lives were lost in this tragedy? Who knows how many brothers and sisters and fathers and mothers will no longer be able to connect with their loved ones? Tomorrow at 8:00 a.m., we will try to explore that question. Until then, hug your loved ones and remind yourself how important they are."

At ten thirty, he walked into his Murray Hill apartment with dust flying off his suit and hugged Mia. With little eloquence, he reminded her how very important she was to his happiness.

The next day, he showed up at 8:00 a.m. with his crew and explained the intended gist of this day. All day long, they would stand at the fence where family members would post pictures of their loved ones who were lost or buried in the collapsed buildings. It was Chaz Conner's least favorite reportage—the need to deal in others' sorrow with very little upside potential. However, from his early days in J-school, he had learned that human interest stories held the biggest sway with audiences.

An emotional father or mother, uncle or aunt, or sister or brother who simply wanted to reconnect one last time with a lost loved one was irresistible. And occasionally, some publicity could actually help relocate the lost soul. Given the fact that Chaz had actually been in the rubble of the collapsed towers, he instinctively knew that the chances were slim. However, voices had been heard under the fallen concrete. Trained dogs were sniffing in every direction. And according to the police, several people had actually been rescued.

Despite his distaste for this reportage, Chaz did find himself emotionally charged with the relatives that he interviewed:

"He is a good man and a good father. I just want people to find him."

"My mom is one who has the best sense of humor, but this is deadly serious."

"He's my brother and a valiant firefighter. I'm sure he climbed up the stairs when everyone else was trying to go down. Can someone not save him?"

"My young daughter had a job interview that morning at the Windows of the World. Here's her picture, in case anyone has seen her."

On the third day, there was some legit news.

The White House claimed there was overwhelming evidence that Osama bin Laden was behind the attack. This generated a string of stories: how he might have planned it, who was involved, and how much training it entailed.

But the biggest story of the day was at ground zero, when President Bush stood on a pile of rubble with a bullhorn and addressed the crowds. At one point, someone in the crowd screamed, "I can't hear you!"

Without missing a beat, the president put the bullhorn to his mouth and screamed back, "I can hear you. The rest of the world hears you. And the people—the people who knocked these buildings down will hear from all of us soon."

With that machismo and bravado, there was massive applause. It was as if this country was suddenly united around a common goal.

On that evening's telecast, Chaz Conner summed it up:

"Today, in the depths of destruction, America held hands and promised to move forward. We learned who our enemies are. We learned what evil they are capable of creating. We learned that we are a strong nation, and that we must defend our values. And what's next? I predict that we will soon learn who our friends are."

In the next six days, Chaz broadcasted every evening from ground zero. On one day, he would salute the firefighters who had come from neighboring communities. On another, he would lionize the health-care workers who were working around the clock to treat the injured. On another, he would showcase the caterers who would provide hot meals outside St. Paul's Chapel.

Throughout these dark days, his marathon broadcasts became the staple of information for all New Yorkers and for the nation. When he wrapped up his last broadcast downtown, he thanked his viewers for tuning in and encouraged them to keep the faith.

"What's next? I have a hunch that we will someday see a silver lining through these gray skies. It might take some sacrifices on our part. It might take a few years. But keep the faith. We have bounced back from Great Depressions and World Wars—and will bounce back from this tragedy as well. It's in our DNA. It's the way we are made. It's what makes this nation special. You know it, and I know it.

"I will see you on the regular broadcasts of *What's Next?* this Wednesday, but we will revisit this scene many times in the months to come—if for no other reason than to let the volunteers down here know that we appreciate their efforts and that this tragedy will never be forgotten."

CHAPTER 26

2008: Hope

"What do you think you will do?" Mia Conner asked her husband, who had decided to step down from the eye of the hurricane after being the omnipresent voice of journalism for almost fifty years. At the age of seventy- seven, he felt it was time to reduce his decades-long anchoring and newsgathering job at ABC. In appreciation of his years of service, his boss, Roone Arledge, had named him anchor emeritus and promised America that Chaz would not be going away. According to Roone, "His appearances at ABC will simply become more special."

In answer to his wife's question, Chaz answered, "I'll do more of what I want to do. Seven or eight special reports a year, most of which I will choose."

"Don't you think you will be bored?"

"I hope not. For one thing, we will have more time to travel and enjoy some dinners without me having to check my cell phone every damn minute to see if I need to get on a plane by 10:50 p.m. I won't have to have a piece of luggage prepacked for the fast getaways. And I won't have to research the entire world hours every day just to be conversant with every newsworthy person on the planet."

"I repeat the question," Mia asked. "Don't you think you will be bored?"

"Not with you at my side, my dear. You have always had a knack for surprising and exciting me." Besides knowing a good line when one popped in his head, Chaz Conner meant it. He had fallen in love with her while she was one of the key attorneys at ABC who protected him against nuisance libel suits from interviewees who believed that Chaz "forced" them to admit things that they subsequently regretted. She had won every case, and the two of them had enjoyed an intellectually and physically satisfying relationship since 1989.

With this new freedom (and as a way to jump-start a change from type-A behavior to type-B behavior), Chaz had scheduled a two-month holiday with Mia.

It centered on three geographical areas that had largely eluded Chaz's news reportage.

The first was Asia. For some reason, his years of news stories never brought him to this neck of the global woods. So for three weeks, the couple would be in Tokyo, Kyoto (via the bullet train), Singapore, and Bangkok, with a coda in Hong Kong.

Verdict: They loved the region, but were ready for a hamburger.

Next stop: Africa. Here they visited Nairobi. They went on a wild game safari. Then on to South Africa, ending up in Marrakech. Along the way, Chaz (from years of journalistic practice) couldn't resist taking notes. Ah, the magnetic twinges of a former life! However, in a bold act of transition, he actually threw his notes in the trash can of his Marrakech hotel room. "Live in the moment." He winked at his wife, and they advanced to the third leg of their around-the-world journey.

Welcome to South America. Here, they fell in love all over again. It started in Buenos Aires (which, at the time, was dubbed the Paris of Latin America). They enjoyed the Argentine beef and the tango, and they even tried it a few times. They then visited Iguazu Falls, one of the absolute wonders of the world, which sits on the border of Argentina, Brazil, and Paraguay. They both agreed it was the most breathtaking site they had ever seen.

From there they moved to Rio, arguably one of the sexiest, most sensual, most artistic cities in the world. It has its own style, its own cuisine. Its own music. Its own world-famous beaches. Its own *chaiprarnyas* ... all of which are easily accessible and relatable to Westerners. Mia and Chaz agreed they could stay at their resort for another month, but decided to complete the trip and return to "normal" life in New York City.

To be perfectly honest, the reentry was jarring. There was the usual rush and push of New Yorkers. But for the Conner couple, it was the bigger dislocation from life at home—Mia had more than three hundred e-mails, most of which were personal in nature. For Chaz, he had never gone so many weeks without input from the wire services or world events. There were about eight hundred messages that should be returned. Within five days, he and Mia returned all the text or e-mail messages.

Within weeks, the news icon agreed to interview with Tom Ridge, the new head of the newly formed Department of Homeland Security. Despite being a bit out of practice, the anchor emeritus did get into the controversies of the new policy and the color-coding of the "threats to our way of life."

"Is it that simple? If we are in red alert, should we find a bomb shelter?"

"No, but we must be vigilant," Tom Ridge responded.

"And if it's yellow, are we allowed to play a softball game in the local park?"

"I would say that even if the color code is yellow, we should still be vigilant."

"So there is no difference between yellow and hot red," Chaz challenged.

"No. One is vigilant. One is more vigilant."

After a three-second pause, Chaz Conner furrowed his brow and admitted to the audience, "Hopefully, you can assess the difference. I cannot. But I do thank Tom Ridge for attempting to exchange the razor-thin difference between yellow and red threat alerts."

Secretary Ridge, a normally nice guy, stormed off the studio with this affront. However, the story stuck and was repeated on many cable channels.

In the ensuing weeks and years, Chaz Conner had exclusive special reports about Saddam Hussein's capture at Tikrit, the Abu Ghraib prison torture, the Statue of Liberty being reopened in 2004, the Scott Peterson-Lacy Peterson murder, the Prince Charles and

Camilla Parker-Bowles wedding, Disneyland's fiftieth anniversary, and an interview with Nancy Pelosi, the first female Speaker of the House.

By late 2007, at the age of eighty-two, Charles announced his formal retirement to ABC with one last proviso and one last assignment—that he could cover the inauguration of the first African-American president ever elected in the United States.

He had admired Barrack Obama since the man's speech at the 2004 Democratic convention, when the Illinois senator gave a stem-winder about his belief that there should be "no Blue States America, no Red States America—just the United States of America." Obama was also ready for a turn on the engagement foreign policy in the US. Chaz had never been a supporter of the war in Iraq, and he was happy to side with someone who wanted to untangle America's military interests.

And then there was the fact that the candidate was black (or at least half- black). Ever since Chaz had served in WWII in segregated corps, he had felt that an unfair hand had been dealt to the blacks in America. He experienced it firsthand when he lived in St. Louis and in Chicago, where ghettos definitely existed. In the sixties, he felt some hope; but over the past three decades, he realized the deep prejudices were ingrained in American society. And yet this amazing candidate held out the promise of a new day.

"What amazing progress this would be," he told his grandson, Louis. "We live a century and a half after the Civil War and still have racial troubles in this country. It makes me sad. If he gets elected, we are definitely going to the historic inaugural."

Lo and behold, Barrack was elected, and Chaz Conner lobbied hard to be the true anchor emeritus and correspondent in chief at the event. He promised the network it would be his last broadcast. He also promised that it would be a doozy.

In the bleachers, there was a bevy of famous people—Jimmy Carter, George H. W. Bush, Bill Clinton, George W. Bush, Walter Mondale, Dan Quayle, Al Gore, Dick Cheney, John Lewis, and more than 180 Tuskegee Airmen.

There was also a large collection of Hollywood glitterati—Beyonce Knowles (who would later sing the Etta James hit "At Last" at one of the inaugural balls), Tiger Woods, Steven Spielberg, James Taylor, Jay-Z, Tom Hanks, Denzel Washington, Dustin Hoffman, and Samuel L. Jackson.

Fact is, there were more than four hundred thousand people around the president-elect on that afternoon. They had followed him on the parade to the White House and sat in reverence when he delivered his address called "A New Birth of Freedom" to the nation and the biggest international audience since the Olympics.

In the late afternoon, after Obama was sworn into office, Chaz Conner took the microphone for the last time. "Today, history was made. Fact is, it is made every time a US president is sworn into office, but this was a rather special inauguration. For the first time, an African-American was sworn into office. It was accompanied by the one and only Aretha Franklin, who sang "My Country, 'Tis of Thee." The invocation was given by the evangelist Rick Warren, and the Bible used for the oath of office was the same exact one used by Abraham Lincoln. How fitting?

"Yesterday, on Martin Luther King Day, thirteen thousand community- service projects took place in the nation. Perhaps that's a testament to a changed nation. Perhaps it will be one where we care a bit more about our fellow man, woman, and neighbor.

"I am here today with my wife, my daughter, my son-in-law, and my grandson to witness this inauguration. I must admit, when I was a young boy, I never imagined such an event could happen in my lifetime. I am so glad to have survived long enough to see it happen. There is no downside to this whatsoever. As I used to sign off in my favorite show *What's Next?* … and as the Beach Boys sing today, 'God only knows.' As Barrack Obama's poster declares: Hope. I will be doing so in the days and months again, and I hope you will be doing the same. Good night and good luck."

With those last words, Chaz's soundman and cameraman motioned that they were off-air, and signaled Mia to enter from the wings with champagne. There were glasses and hugs for everyone, including a few correspondents from competing networks who were full of kudos for the man they all respected. Amidst the bubble, the news fraternity all admitted that this was an amazing, extraordinary moment.

"Why? Because I am leaving the fold and contributing ratings to you," Chaz teased Dan Rather—whom, despite several teams, he always liked because of his wit and his drive.

"Yes, partly." Rather raised his glass to Chaz. "But also because we are now a post-racial society."

"Not so fast, Dan," Chaz responded like a wise uncle. "Yep, this is a big moment. No question about it. But we still have miles ahead of us. Let's see how it unfolds in the years to come."

"I hope it's good," Rather answered with optimism.

"As do I," Chaz rejoined as they clinked glasses.

Later on that night, Chaz's grandson, Lew, knocked on the door of his grandfather's hotel room. Chaz opened the door and saw the young man standing in the hallway. Of course, he immediately invited the boy in.

"I can't begin to tell you how moved I was by the inauguration and by your last words on TV. And I wanted to give you a gift to commemorate this event." The grandson then extended a scroll to Chaz.

"Should I open it now?" the grandfather asked.

"Maybe tomorrow," the kid said. "But I predict you will like it."

When Chaz unfolded the scroll in front of Mia, he honestly wept. It was Obama's ever-present campaign poster in red, beige, and dark blue that was created by Shephard Fairey. It showed the candidate (now the president) looking skyward. At the bottom of the page was the simple sans-serif word: *Hope.*

CHAPTER 27

2015: The End

For the first time in more than eight decades, Chaz Conner began to feel that he was actually slowing down. No, this was different from when he was simply in his late seventies and wanted to slow down his work schedule. At this point, in his late eighties, he actually felt that he moved slower. In a city like New York, that's a problem. The mad dash to get from point A to point B a few seconds sooner than the same trek yesterday is irresistible to most Manhattanites. When an old codger gets in the way, it's irritating. We tend to want to just knock him or her down and tell them to "get out of the way." Instead, we normally just storm by, turn our heads in disgust, roll our eyes, and sigh loudly enough to be heard by the slow-moving fart.

For the past few years, Chaz Conner had experienced this phenomenon. For the longest time, he simply blamed it on old age (an astute observation, at age 89). However, in the last few months, he felt that his pace was decreasing even more rapidly. Even his wife had noticed the change in his tempo. Consequently, rather than walk to and from all their favorite destinations, she often suggested that they take more übercars to and from restaurants and theaters. Make note: they did not decrease their exposure to Broadway or French cafés.

Their favorites of the past few years were *Jersey Boys*, *The Book of Mormon*, and *Fun Home*. Sometimes, they would see a show with his daughter Serena and her husband, Tom, along with his grandson, Louis. Chaz particularly loved these evenings since it gave him a chance to catch up on family news.

On this particular afternoon, they were having lunch at Joe Allen's, before a Saturday matinee of *Kinky Boots*. It was always one of Chaz Conner's favorite theatrical restaurants. For one thing, it was close to all the major theaters. All the waiters were out-of-work actors. Many of the Broadway stars would visit there after a show. The food was acceptable, not great—but you always felt that you were in the epicenter of song and dance, drama, and comedy.

After hugs and kisses, the family settled down to drinks and snacks.

"I'm looking forward to this afternoon—partly because I am with my favorite people, and partly because I met Cyndi Lauper in my coverage of "We Are the World." She was a little weirdo then, but had loads of talent, and I predict we will see both this afternoon. Cheers." He raised his glass and clinked with everyone, including his grandson, Louis, who had ginger ale.

After some small talk, the conversation moved into meatier matters.

Chaz learned that Tom had been promoted as the office manager at Merrill Lynch.

"Congratulations, I guess. Does that mean you will cease giving stock advice to individuals that have trusted you for years? Will you now just manage employees?"

Tom answered the question and instinctively knew his father-in-law would like the answer. "It just means more hours. I stipulated that I wanted to retain my portfolio of important clients, many of whom are widows and would be discombobulated with a change of stewardship."

Chaz smiled and then looked at his grandson. "Lewis, do you understand the word 'discombobulated'?"

"Messed up?" the kid asked.

"Close enough," Chaz answered. "By the way, Tom, that is an honorable decision. And you, my dear Serena, what are you up to?"

"I am getting bored as a high school guidance counselor. I think I may want to go back to grad school and figure out a different path."

"Such as?"

"Music therapy is the new thing. Or young-people cancer therapy. Or, more dangerously, criminal or drug-related therapy. I just want to figure out a new path."

Chaz mentally chewed on this and then responded as a sage. "If you feel in your heart and soul, you need a change, you definitely must change. By the way, you really sound like your mother a few decades ago. I assume you stay in contact. How is she?"

"She's good. She's alone now but seems to be happy with her job at the Chicago Institute of Art, where she continues to teach a class each week on the psychological implication of the great masters. I've attended the lectures, they're quite good."

"And what about you, Mia?" Serena asked, partly due to her desire to change the subject from Chaz's first true love, first wife, and mother of his children.

Mia took a sip of her white wine and answered the question, "I am extremely happy at this stage of my life. In the past twelve months, I have given lectures on the 'One-Day University' program on the topic of libel. I have a wonderful man who wishes to see me smile every day. He has a wonderful family sitting around this table. And my dear man continues to agitate ABC news to get on the biggest stories of the week. Once a journalist, always a journalist."

After a few entrées, Chaz realized he had not heard from his grandson. "Lewis, what about you? I know you are only fourteen years old, but what do you think you might want to do in the next ten, twenty, or thirty years?"

"Not sure," the fourteen-year-old responded.

"I understand. But take a wild guess," Grandpa advised.

"I like to write," the kid answered.

After a five-second pause, the veteran journalist looked toward the heavens and his own history. "You will never find a finer profession," he told his grandson. "If you choose to write for a living, I want you to have the Waterman pen my mother gave me when I chose to chronicle the times. Mia, you know where it is. Maybe you can find it, and make sure it is delivered to Lewis. It has the potential to write good things." The grandfather winked at the kids.

The rest of the lunch was sweetness and light. Lots of laughs. Inevitably, a bit of politics. Lots of irony, a few laughs about last week's *Saturday Night Live*, and the surreal comedy called *Birdman*.

Thirty minutes before the start of the matinee, Chaz asked for a check, offered his American Express, and signed the bill.

Halfway down the block, on the way to *Kinky Boots* at the Hirschfield Theatre on West Forty-Fifth, Chaz Conner grabbed his chest in agony and crashed to the ground.

Within seconds, Mia had called 911, and the ambulance came to their location. It would take more than twenty minutes for the ambulance to get to their locale at Eighth Avenue. Lesson from this: Try not to have a heart attack in the middle of the theater rush hour in Manhattan.

Within fifty-two minutes, the ambulance arrived at Lennox Hill, and he was rushed into the ER. Over the next hour, it was touch and go. Of course, it came with limited information in this age of medical litigation. No one would admit the extent of the heart damage, or the prognosis for survival. It's far easier from a legal point to simply say, "Hey, what happens, happens."

Twelve hours later, Chaz Conner, with wires attached to both arms and his head, seemed to recognize his wife and family around him. Despite a lifetime of lucidity, he was groggy from the drugs and very bleary eyed. He looked at Mia and said, "I love you." He then reiterated his request at Joe Allen's restaurant, "Give young Louis the Waterman pen my mom gave me. Tell him to write something wonderful."

He then faded in and out of consciousness. Throughout this ordeal, Mia held his limp hand that sometimes felt as if it had life—and sometimes it would feel as if he had passed.

In one last journalistic bottom line, he looked at his wife with flickering eyes and whispered, "What's next?" Then he peacefully closed his eyes and moved on to the next unknown episode.

ACKNOWLEDGMENTS

I'd like to thank some people who helped me with background information on the eras: Brian Goodall, who helped inform me on what it was like to attend Missouri School of Journalism. Rob Conrad, whose knowledge of Chicago was invaluable. Geraldine Seidel, who filled in the blanks about life in the thirties, forties, and fifties … and childbirth. Abby Connett, who gave me some insights about the broadcast news business. And to everyone else who encouraged me along the way, including my children.

Thank you.

OTHER BOOKS BY JOHN NIEMAN

Novels
The Wrong Number One
Blue Morpho
Close Call

Children's Books
The Amazing Rabbitini
Kids from A to Z

Short-Story Collections
Three-Minute Shorts
Art with a Story
Art with a Story 2

Art Books
Art of Lists
Art of More Lists
Art of Even More Lists
Art of Lists IV

Art and Essays
What Is Missing?
The Wanted Book